SPEAKING
FROM
EXPERIENCE

Illustrated solutions to
the business problems
you face every day.

Based on the works
of L.Ron Hubbard

Concept Technologies, Inc.

Published by Concept Technologies, Inc.
200 North Maryland Avenue, Suite 301, Glendale, California 91206

© 1996, 1999, 2001, 2004, 2007, 2010, 2012 Concept Technologies, Inc. All Rights Reserve

Library of Congress No. 95-74963

ISBN 0-9648491-0-0

12 11 10 9 8 7

Printed in China.

In reading this book, be very certain you never go past a word you do not fully understand.

The only reason a person gives up a study or becomes confused or unable to learn is because he or she has gone past a word which was not understood.

The confusion or inability to grasp or learn comes AFTER a word that the person did not have defined or understood.

Therefore, in studying this book be very, very certain you never go past a word you do not fully understand. If the material becomes confusing or you can't seem to grasp it, there will be a word just earlier that you have not understood. Don't go any further, but go back to the area BEFORE you got into trouble, find the misunderstood word and get it defined.

Note: As an aid to the reader, a glossary is included at the back of this book which defines the words which are most likely to be misunderstood. Words sometimes have several meanings. The glossary definitions in this book only give the meaning of the word as it is used in the text. Other definitions for the word can be found in a dictionary.

Table of Contents

Introduction

Introduction

Speaking From Experience will dramatically increase anyone's basic understanding of groups and how they work. While this is primarily a book on *management*, it will broaden one's perspective in numerous ways.

The principles contained in this book are based on extensive research into the subjects of management, organization, people and their work. It outlines certain laws of management which are uniform and unchanging in any group endeavor. This material is currently being used in many highly successful corporations around the world.

The illustrated situations found in these pages were not "dreamed up in order to tell a good story"; they are based on practical everyday experiences.

This book is quite different from other books on management in that each page covers a single concept, presented in an illustrated fashion. This helps the reader to cut quickly through the words and directly into the conceptual understanding of the subject matter. But don't let yourself be fooled by its apparent simplicity. When simplicity and truth are combined, the results are very powerful.

Regardless of the condition of the economy, a well-managed organization will flourish and prosper, whereas a poorly-managed organization will tend to collapse. The ability to make a business successful under *any* economic condition stems from a keen understanding of management itself.

In truth, there is a phenomenal difference between expert management and poor management. It is a difference which can almost single-handedly change the course of an entire culture.

When L. Ron Hubbard began to examine the problems of organization and management in the early 1950s, the serious lack of workable systems soon became obvious. This led him to begin an active search for basic laws governing the survival and expansion of all organizations and groups.

As a result of this search, he isolated for the first time, the skills that a man or woman needs to succeed. And with his keen understanding of life's fundamentals, he discovered and codified simple and practical steps through which one can sanely and easily create an expanding and enduring organization.

"Organization is actually a simple subject," he wrote in 1969, "based on a few basic patterns which, if applied, produce success."

Whether your company or business is large or small, you will find that through the use of L. Ron Hubbard's management and administrative technology, you will have within your grasp the tools of limitless success and expansion.

Mr. Hubbard was a man of amazing accomplishment. Although many of his years were spent in the development of Scientology®, it was only one facet of his incredible contribution to mankind. His researches led him to the discovery of fundamentals in many, many areas of life, from education and drug rehabilitation to self-help and personal improvement. Many corporations, businesses and individuals have benefited from his technologies.

Management

The Seminar

Meet Thomas Bradford and Janet Mitchel.

Hello. For those of you who are new here today, my name is Thomas Bradford and this is my associate, Janet Mitchel. We are management consultants who specialize in the management techniques researched and developed by L. Ron Hubbard. It is an exact technology which is based on the fundamental laws of groups and group activities.

Today's seminar covers a broad spectrum of business management principles. I understand that we have quite a diverse audience here today including professionals from many different industries and business sectors. Even though your own specific job titles and responsibilities may vary, you will find that every concept we present has a direct impact upon the success of your group or company.

Throughout this book, Thomas and Janet will be giving an in-depth, comprehensive management seminar to their new and existing clients. When Thomas and Janet speak the text is always blue. A client's input is green. General text (narration) is black. As you read, consider yourself part of the audience.

Getting Started!

During today's seminar we will be using scenes from some of our clients' businesses to demonstrate the management tools we will be discussing. As we begin the seminar you may feel that certain parts of what we are covering are "very basic"; however, we strongly recommend against assuming that you "already know" this material. As you read, you will discover various management concepts which are indeed exciting, clear, bold and *new*.

We will start with the fundamentals that form the backbone of any organized activity and use them much like a builder uses a proper foundation in constructing a sound building.

We will be covering a fair amount in a relatively short period of time, so please feel free to ask questions. Enjoy the seminar!

The concepts discussed in the first few sections form the basis for more advanced management techniques found later in the book. Therefore, in reading this book it is important to start from the beginning of the text and read all the way through. You will find the pages interesting and quick to read.

Let's get right into it. Many of you feel that your company or group is *not* operating at its fullest potential. You are right. This seminar will help orient you to those areas of management you must know more about in order to achieve immediate yet long-lasting improvement.

The total and complete purpose of managing anything is to guide and direct its activities in order to achieve its fullest potential.

Note: The principles of management described in this seminar are true for a business, yet they are equally applicable to managing a household.

11

The Existing Scene

As a manager, you constantly handle both good and bad situations.

The term **Existing Scene** refers to what is happening *now*. It may be totally acceptable...

...or it may be disastrous.

The current situation in a business, whatever it may be, is referred to as the existing scene.

Managers are there to ensure that the existing scene *improves*. In fact, the sole responsibility of management is to understand how and why good or bad situations exist, and to then bring the scene closer to the ideals which have been envisioned for the group or activity.

The Science of Management

Management is a science governed by specific principles and procedures which, if applied, will improve the existing scene resulting in a highly successful business. This book covers the science of management in a way that everyone can understand.

The Scale of Administration

One of our clients is an environmental specialty firm named Clean Horizons, Inc. When we first started consulting them, we found that they had a strong vision of their goal, but, in truth, the company was getting nowhere. They had many diverse, unorganized and uncoordinated projects, each of which sounded great, but upon closer inspection were found to be producing little. The company as a whole had never pulled together into a tightly organized, efficient team.

We employed a top-to-bottom comprehensive organizational method which turned Clean Horizons, Inc. into a well-managed, profitable and expanding operation which has a great future.

In the following pages Thomas and Janet describe the management techniques which were used to turn Clean Horizons around.

The Admin Scale

In order to sort out Clean Horizons' internal confusions, Thomas and Janet helped them get organized with the use of an **Admin* Scale** as follows.

The Admin Scale is a guide used to establish and align the activities inherent in any successful organization.

The Admin Scale

Goals
Purposes
Policy
Plans
Programmes
Projects
Orders
Ideal Scenes
Statistics
Valuable Final Products

A conceptual tool has been discovered by Mr. Hubbard called the Admin Scale. It gives a sequence and relative seniority of subjects relating to organization. The Admin Scale is a fantastically powerful tool. It is far more than just a list of business topics.

* Note: ("Admin" is short for administration).

We thoroughly addressed each one of the points on the scale within Clean Horizons and will be discussing each one of them here today.

The Admin Scale

Goals
Purposes
Policy
Plans
Programmes
Projects
Orders
Ideal Scenes
Statistics
Valuable Final Products

The full ability to utilize the Admin Scale comes from an understanding of each of its items as well as the inter-relationships between them.

Goals

Goals are the most senior item of the scale. They are paramount in any endeavor and, whether stated or not, every activity has a goal. Clean Horizons' is shown here.

Sample Goal

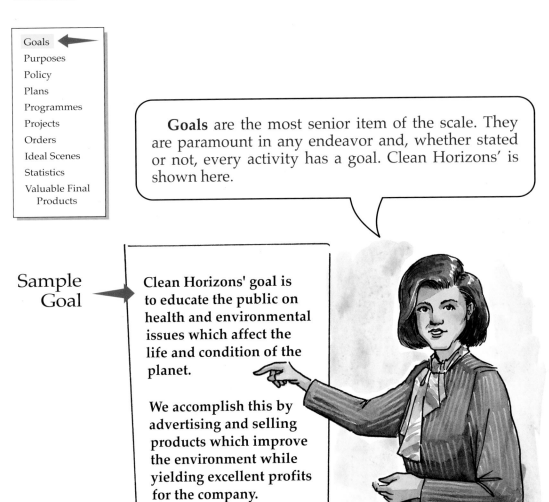

Clean Horizons' goal is to educate the public on health and environmental issues which affect the life and condition of the planet.

We accomplish this by advertising and selling products which improve the environment while yielding excellent profits for the company.

A goal is the overall concept of what one intends to accomplish.

A goal is a dream or a vision of a desirable future that is put forth and that acts as an overall guide regarding the activities of a person or group.

The scope of a goal may vary; however, a properly stated goal for any group must be broad enough to encompass all of its basic activities.

Purposes

A well-stated goal should be accompanied by a variety of associated **purposes**.

Each purpose must align with the goal. Here are some of Clean Horizons' purposes which forward their goal.

GOAL: Clean Horizons' goal is to educate the public on health and environmental issues which affect the life and condition of our planet. This is accomplished by advertising and selling products which improve...

PURPOSE: To develop and broadly market products which greatly reduce air pollution.

PURPOSE: To purify drinking waters in ways which are safe and economical for broad use.

PURPOSE: To develop and broadly market cosmetic and hygiene products that are made from natural ingredients.

Align

Goals and purposes are general statements which do not contain highly detailed descriptions. Purposes address more specific subjects or activities than goals. Goals are of greater importance.

Policy is a set of rules or guidelines by which a group conducts its affairs in order to achieve its goals and purposes. Below are just a few of the policies Clean Horizons wrote and issued.

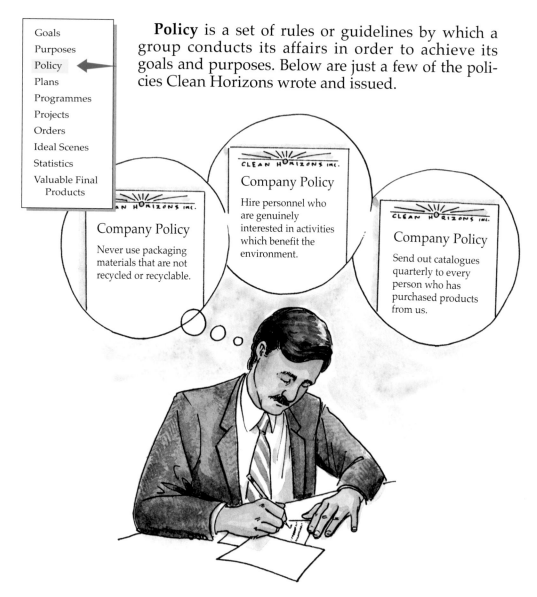

CLEAN HORIZONS INC.

Company Policy

Never use packaging materials that are not recycled or recyclable.

CLEAN HORIZONS INC.

Company Policy

Hire personnel who are genuinely interested in activities which benefit the environment.

CLEAN HORIZONS INC.

Company Policy

Send out catalogues quarterly to every person who has purchased products from us.

Strong policy is derived from successful experience in forwarding a basic purpose, overcoming opposition or enemies, ending distractions and letting the basic purpose flow and expand.

Policy laid down which is thought up independent of experience in similar situations is either the result of great foresight and is successful or it is simply stupidity, in that it seeks to handle situations which will never exist or, if they do, won't be important.

23

Teamwork

When no policy at all exists, random policy occurs. When policy exists but is not known, random policy setting will occur. Ignorance of policy, the need and function of it, can cause random policies. Hidden not stated random policies can conflict.

Random policy is seldom "set" with the group's true goals and purposes in mind, thus opening the door to organizational conflict and destruction.

I've been running this department for years. Things are doing just fine!

I've been transferred to this department for a reason and this isn't how I do things!!!

A group acts as a true team:

- When the individual members understand and fully support the group's basic goals and purposes, and

- When they know and apply the policies of the group.

Purpose is Senior to Policy

The following is an example of how a policy that runs contrary to purpose can cause trouble.

I don't understand why it is company policy to send out catalogues every two years. The sales are always much better right after a mailing. We should send them out every 3 months.

CLEAN HORIZONS INC.

Policy

Clean Horizons is to have a constantly expanding customer base therefore catalogues are to be sent every two years.

Purpose is senior to policy (as listed on the Admin Scale). Even though it is extremely important to follow a group's policies, it makes no sense to "follow a policy" that does not produce results needed to forward the goals and purposes of the group.

Plans

A **plan** is an outline of the general actions which a group must execute in order to achieve its goals. Good planning is always done in accordance with policy.

Here is a very successful plan that we helped Clean Horizons outline.

PLAN

Utilize our catalogue marketing activities to keep our clients abreast of new environmental safety tips. Test a series of marketing campaigns for our newest products using television commercials. Each campaign will be built around the strategic use of catalogue mailings to our entire customer base. The commercials will expand our customer base while our highly informative catalogues increase orders from existing customers.

Planning is key to successful management. The effective use of the Admin Scale serves to ensure that the goals, purposes, policy and planning of a group continually align.

A **strategic plan** is a statement of intended plans for accomplishing a broad objective. It is the central strategy worked out at the top which, like an umbrella, covers the activities of the echelons below it.

Strategic planning provides direction for the activities of all the lower echelons. To be effective, this planning must be done with a complete overview of the existing scene.

Programmes

A **programme*** is a series of steps in the correct sequence necessary to carry out a plan. A plan has to exist in a person's mind, whether written or not, before a programme can be written.

Sample Programme ➤

Marketing Programme

Each step of this programme must be completed before the video tests are considered 100% complete. The purpose of the programme is to ensure that each segment of our commercials achieves the correct response for our target audience. The purpose of our commercials is to attract new customers; therefore our videos must be tested on persons who have never used our products.

Read the entire programme before beginning its execution. Please sign and date each programme step when completed.

Target #1 New Product Video Test

Target #2 Revise Internal Marketing Policies

Target #3 Develop Commercials

Target #4 Broadcast the Commercials

Target #5 Implement Quarterly Catalogue Mailings

Here you see one of the programmes Clean Horizons used to carry out its plan.

Note: The British spelling of "programme" is used here so as not to be confused with a computer "program".

Goals
Purposes
Policy
Plans
Programmes
Projects ◀
Orders
Ideal Scenes
Statistics
Valuable Final
 Products

Programmes may be further broken down into **projects**.

Sample Project

Marketing programme target #1: New Product Video Test

(**Project 1.1: Selection of a Video House**)

Responsible Person: Horace Smith   Date completed: ___ / ___ / ___

Clean Horizons must locate a top quality video production house to help develop the segments that will be tested.

A. Develop a list of video production houses whose videos have had superior customer response ratings.

B. Interview the top 4 video houses.

C. Closely inspect their work.   Collect video samples.

D. Submit your recommendation of the best video house. Include supporting material to back up your decision.

E. Set up a meeting with the Clean Horizons' Vice President of Marketing to finalize the selection.

This project must be completed within 2 weeks.

A project is the sequence of steps written to carry out one step of a programme.

Tactical Planning

From the strategic plan, **tactical planning** would be done, taking the broad strategic targets and breaking them down into precise and exactly-targeted actions (programmes and projects).

When the strategic plan, with its purpose, has been put forward, it is picked up by the next lower level of management and turned into tactical planning.

Note: The term *strategy* here refers to the broad fashion of how things are to be conducted whereas *tactics* refers to specific and immediate objectives.

Plans, Programmes and Projects

Plans and Programmes may span many months or years, while projects generally require significantly less time.

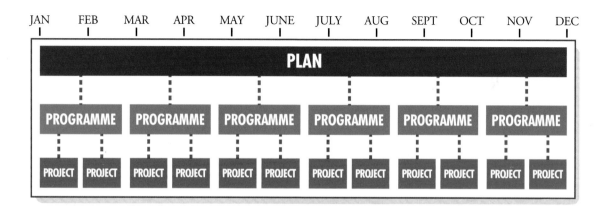

Completed projects lead to completed programmes which lead to completed plans which in turn lead to significant advances toward the group's goals and purposes.

Note: Plans are sometimes referred to as "Strategic Plans", "Business Plans", "5 Year Plans", etc.

Battle Plans

Tactical planning consists of **battle plans** (**BP**s). A BP is sometimes referred to as a game plan. A BP is a list of targets for the coming day or week which forwards the strategic plan and handles the immediate factors which impede it.

A battle plan is more than just an "Action Plan" or a "To Do" list. Its actions align with the strategies of the group.

The purpose of organization is to make planning an actuality. In order to accomplish this, a manager must see that his personnel's battle plans are coordinated as well as completed. Such team coordination often occurs in meetings reviewing daily or weekly battle plans.

Without coordination the various actions of the organization can get crossed and wind up in a confused, unproductive mess.

Battle Plans and Strategic Plans

There is one thing to beware of in doing battle plans. One can write a great many targets which have little or nothing to do with the strategic plan yet keep people terribly busy and which accomplish no part of the overall strategic plan. Thus a battle plan can become a liability since it isn't pushing any overall strategic plan and is not accomplishing any tactical objective.

Battle plans must always be written and coordinated to accomplish a specific part of the overall strategy.

Orders involve specific actions which get things done. They can and should be done in a short period of time (NOW).

Order

Send these toothpaste samples to our test market survey team in Chicago.

Some programme steps are so simple that they themselves are an order.

If a business is to run smoothly, the lower points of the Admin Scale (such as plans, programmes, projects and orders) must align with the more senior items on the scale.

Ideal Scenes

The **ideal scene** is the vision of the way a business or any of its parts "ideally ought to be." A description of an ideal scene always coincides 100% with the goals and purposes of an activity. It is what one is striving to achieve.

Policy expressing the Ideal Scene

CLEAN HORIZONS INC.

POLICY
Catalogue Shipping

Clean Horizons is to have a constantly expanding well-informed customer base who are regularly updated regarding any new product release as well as our complete environmentally safe product line. Catalogues are to be sent every month.

The ideal scene includes details not specifically described by the goals and purposes. Contained in a group's policies should be a description of its goals, purposes *and* the ideal scene for each of its activities.

It is usually very easy to understand a group's goals and purposes. However, in order to truly know the ideal scene for a group or any of its areas one must have a close working knowledge and familiarity of how it "ought to function."

Many outside observers (or even an area's own managers) can make errors in their judgement by conceiving of an "ideal" that is actually unrealistic and inappropriate for that activity.

Statistics (Stats)

A statistic is a number or amount compared to an earlier number or amount of the same thing.

Statistics refer to the quantity of work done or the value of it in money. The stat, if properly stated and honestly kept, is a vital indicator of the scene.

The lowly "art" of falsifying statistics is common in this society. Management by statistics is not a game of cover-up and make believe based on apparencies or politics. You will find that the proper use of the statistics we are describing will lead to an increase in productivity.

Any Activity can Have a Statistic

Any experienced manager will agree that business management is a subject of how to get results. Therefore, the following is an inescapable fact: If you are responsible for getting results you've got to be able to properly measure them. Problems in productivity are much more easily resolved when the ongoing results are being accurately measured.

Each activity of an organization should have a statistic which represents the quantity or value of its results.

Some have argued that it is either impractical or impossible to track a stat for certain types of key production areas in a group. The best managers do not give in to that argument. In fact they proceed to identify the most appropriate statistics and get them tracked.

Up Statistic

When the quantity of production increases (as shown on the graph) it is called an **up statistic**.

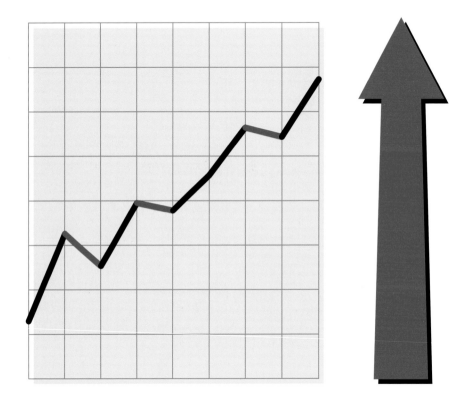

Very simply, this means that more results have been achieved within that section or department of the organization.

When the quantity of production decreases it is called a **down statistic**.

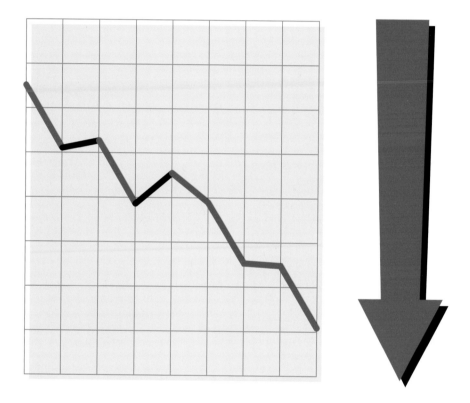

When statistics are down, you know that something is wrong and must be handled.

"Upside Down" Graphs

Some stats should be graphed upside down. For example, suppose the increase in a certain statistic would represent bad news and a decrease would be good news. This would have to be graphed differently than other graphs.

Upside Down Statistic

#of Product Refunds

When graphing results for management purposes, up should always be good and down should be bad. So, the rule is this: if you want less of something, graph it upside down.

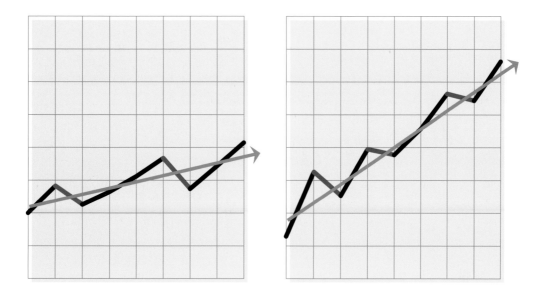

Trends

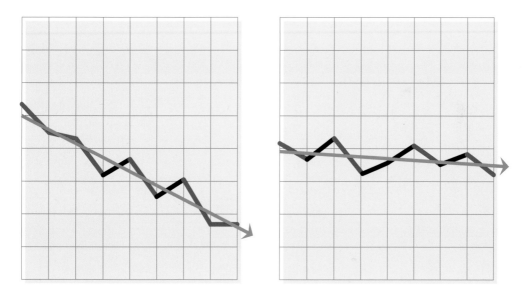

A **trend** is the overall measure of expansion (production) or contraction (non-production) and is the most valuable message to be obtained from a statistic.

Performance on the Job

Once each activity of the organization has a statistic that accurately measures the production of that area, one can immediately see how productive it has been by viewing the stats.

Statistics and the Ideal Scene

Goals
Purposes
Policy
Plans
Programmes
Projects
Orders
Ideal Scenes
Statistics
Valuable Final
 Products

**Correct
Statistic**

The correct statistic for an area is one that, if increased, moves the activity closer to its ideal scene.

Valuable Final Products

All businesses provide products (either goods or services) which have value to others. A **valuable final product** (or **VFP**) is a *completed* product.

Here are some of Clean Horizons' VFPs.

We don't just call them goods and services. We call them valuable final products because that is what must be produced. A VFP is *valuable* because it can be exchanged with others who need or want the product. It is *final* because it is <u>done</u>.

46

VFPs are the end result of an activity. The production of specific, definable VFPs is the reason a business, group or activity exists as an organized unit.

Something which is partially done, incomplete or not able to be used is *not* a VFP.

When the importance of VFPs is clearly understood, things run well; when it isn't, things can go downhill quickly.

Goals and Valuable Final Products

The valuable final products of an organization or activity must align with its goals and purposes.

Although the VFP is listed at the bottom of the scale, the quality, reliability and usefulness of a group's VFP is fantastically important to a group's continued survival.

Aligning each Item on the Admin Scale

The Admin Scale is for use. It is worked up and down until it is (each item) in full agreement with the remaining items.

When an item in the scale is *not* aligned with the other items, the activity will be hindered if not fail.

The Admin Scale

Goals

Purposes

Policy

Plans

Programmes

Projects

Orders

Ideal Scenes

Statistics

Valuable Final Products

Groups appear slow, inefficient, unhappy, inactive or quarrelsome only when these items are not aligned, made known and coordinated.

Any activity can be improved by debugging or aligning this scale in relation to the group activity. The skill with which all these items in any activity are aligned and gotten into action is called *management*.

The Admin Scale in Action

VFPs

Ideal Scene

Order

Project

Policy

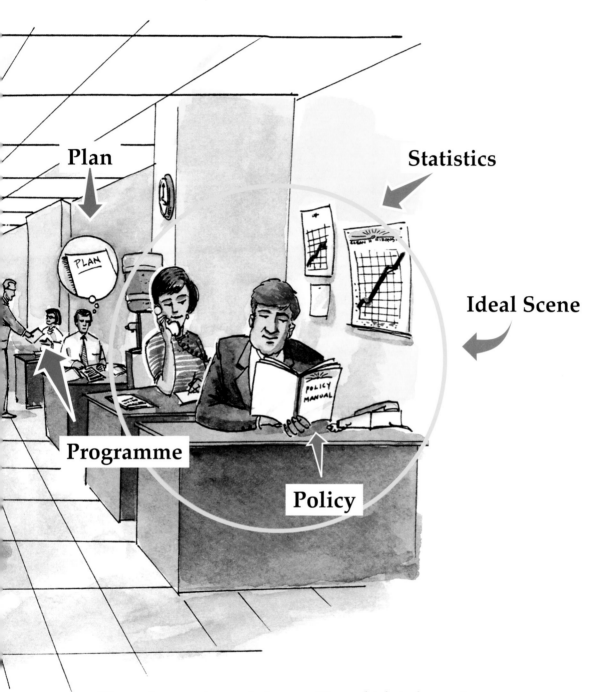

Plan

Statistics

Ideal Scene

Programme

Policy

It's a pleasure to work in an office which is humming away with all ten points of the Admin Scale in full use! You can see here that the Admin Scale is not just information written down on a piece of paper and left to collect dust. It is a dynamic tool which applies to every aspect of an organization.

If fully understood and properly used, the Admin Scale is possibly the single most powerful tool in business management because it addresses every aspect of any organization, large or small.

The principles of the Admin Scale are basic and will work regardless of the activity's product or purpose. However, this book was written with the sole intention that it be used for activities which in some way benefit mankind.

As you and your associates work with the concepts of the Admin Scale, your appreciation for its true brilliance will strengthen. It is indeed comprehensive.

You will find it valuable to re-read the Admin Scale section at a later date. But before you do, take a look at the businesses you deal with every day (including your own). Compare the existing scene, point by point on the scale, with the way things ought to be in that company. Do the plans make complete sense? Do all the points of the scale actually align within the company? Does each policy really work? Are production statistics tracked or does it remain unclear whether or not certain vital actions are completed? These are very important questions. Your answer to each one will greatly improve when you put the Admin Scale into use.

Note: The construction of this book is similar to the way blocks are used in a building. The Admin Scale is part of the foundation. The following sections of this book continually refer back to the basics found in this scale.

Production and and Exchange

Customer satisfaction is based upon delivering high-quality valuable final products (VFPs). This is immediately apparent in the restaurant business. Here you see Christopher's Golden Nugget which is owned and operated by Christopher Donaldson. He is here today at the seminar. Christopher came to us for help. He wanted more clients. In his business, word of mouth is everything so we focused on improving the production and exchange in his restaurant.

The following pages include scenes from Christopher's Golden Nugget which describe the basic yet powerful principles of production and exchange.

Value

Customers who frequent Christopher's Golden Nugget want more than just a meal. The woman here wants great-tasting food and her husband wants it in a timely manner. The fact that they are getting what they want has *value*. While this concept may be "very simple and basic," a group must *never* lose touch with the depth of the word *value*.

VALUE

VALUE

I'm glad I don't have to cook dinner...and the food looks great!

Wow, that was quick!

All businesses are based upon the principle of providing things that are needed and wanted. Anything which is needed and wanted has value (meaning it is worth something to someone). Therefore, in order for something to be a valuable final product, it must have value.

Products and Sub-Products

Here we see Thomas helping Christopher clearly define the activities which lead to his restaurant's VFPs.

The waitress takes the order (sub-product); then the chef prepares it (sub-product). As soon as it's ready the waitress serves it (sub-product) and so on until the VFP is achieved, which is a very satisfied customer who has left a nice tip and has fully paid for the meal.

SUB-PRODUCT

SUB-PRODUCT

SUB-PRODUCT

SUB-PRODUCT

Each part of a production sequence is called a **sub-product**. There are often many steps which go into the completion of a single VFP. The sub-products in themselves have relative value. A vital approach towards organizing anything is to clearly define the VFPs and then work backwards defining each sub-product.

Exchange

The word **exchange** has several meanings. Here exchange is defined as the process of offering something valuable in return for some other valuable.

The principles of exchange underlie all organizational activities. A group offers its VFPs to customers in exchange for valuables (usually money as shown above).

It is important to know that exchange does not always involve money as one of the valuables. For example, someone may offer their help regarding one activity in exchange for help on some other activity.

Christopher's Golden Nugget, like any business, survives upon its ability to adequately sell and deliver its products.

A person or group buys a product because they believe they will get what they need and want from it. The entire process of sales and delivery is an agreement (or pact) made with the customer. It is perhaps the most important "contract" in business and must not be violated.

In the illustration above, the customer expects a great meal.

Agreements

People do not always honor their agreements. Businesses do not always provide the product quality that is expected.

Personnel (such as the chef shown here) may or may not provide the quantity or quality of results expected of them.

The nature of an employee's sub-products, whether good or bad, affects the group's VFPs, which in turn affects the reputation and future success of the organization.

Always deliver what was promised.

The factors of *exchange* between a group and its public are accomplished only by delivery.

Hubbard® Management Consultants (such as Thomas and Janet) stress the fact that the above maxim should be adopted by any organization.

The Conditions of Exchange

Please remember that we have many different types of professionals in the seminar audience today. Even though we are using Christopher's restaurant to show you examples, the concepts we are covering regarding production and exchange refer to every type of business. They apply to one's own job or to a group as a whole. Some people always find a way to produce excellent results. Let's take a look at the four basic ways a waitress can handle exchange with customers.

**Four Conditions
of Exchange:**

1. Criminal Exchange

2. Partial Exchange

3. Fair Exchange

4. Exchange in Abundance

The four **conditions of exchange** (as listed above) are described in the following pages.

Criminal Exchange

Here is an example of the lowest level of exchange.

You over-charged me for three different items here! This seems to be a constant problem at this restaurant...

Criminal exchange is taking something for nothing. There is no real exchange involved. An employee that does not carry out his duties but collects a paycheck is an example of criminal exchange. An organization that collects fees for a service or product and never delivers is also criminal.

Partial Exchange

While **partial exchange** is above criminal exchange, it is not at all acceptable in business or in everyday life.

Partial exchange is the act of delivering less than what was agreed upon or expected. This can involve the delivery of only part of the product, a flawed product, or a product which is not completely functional.

Here things are looking better...

Fair exchange involves selling and collecting money for a specific product or service and delivering exactly what has been sold. Most successful businesses and activities operate on the basis of fair exchange.

Exchange in Abundance

Now this is the ideal scene!

This is my favorite restaurant! The service is always great.

Exchange in abundance is the highest condition of exchange. This does not mean one undercharges or gives products or services away. It does mean that one (in some way) delivers something more valuable than the buyer paid for or expected. Unfortunately this condition of exchange is not common.

Exchange involves valuables for valuables. In life, exchange occurs in many ways. A business generally receives money in exchange for a VFP; however, the principles of exchange apply to friendship, sports, goodwill or church activities as well as business transactions. People exchange with their family, friends and country as well as with their business.

You can exchange in abundance with your husband, wife, children, parents and employees, or perhaps you could provide a worthwhile exchange to mankind in general. Truthfully, there is no real limit to the valuable things you can provide.

In summary, regarding the levels or conditions of exchange:

- When operating at the level of criminal exchange, the bigger the group, the longer it takes for it to fall, but fall it assuredly does.

- Partial exchange can only go on so long because eventually the organization or activity will collapse.

- Fair exchange gives one a rather level progress. It is considered honest. It is socially acceptable and very legal under law. It does not, however, guarantee any expansion or improvement of a group.

- The fourth condition (exchange in abundance) is almost unknown. Yet it is the key to howling success and expansion.

Finance and Solvency

Janet kicks off the next session.

We are scheduled to cover many areas of business today. Let's move straight into our next topic; Finance.

Finance and accounting are not the same thing. Finance is senior to accounting. We will not be talking about accounting. We are going to be addressing financial basics which apply to every business professional here.

Our consulting firm has conducted many surveys over the years regarding organizational finance. It's amazing how many businesses, large and small, go through time periods where income is extremely high, but the owners find they did not turn a profit and have little to show for their hard work. This is unnecessary and avoidable.

Rigorous use of the following principles will help companies steer clear of many financial problems.

Solvency (Income greater than Outgo)

The basic rule of **solvency** is "income must be greater than outgo."

One of our clients, Clark's Software, is a successful software company. Clark's was once insolvent, but is now very profitable (solvent). These graphs of income vs. outgo show the difference.

The survival of any organization depends upon *solvency*.

Money

Money represents goods and services. It is a *symbol* which represents the value of goods and services.

Value

While there are many things in this society which seem to indicate otherwise, money has value only because of the goods and services that are made available. This has always been the case and always will be. This is the underlying principle of small companies as well as global economics.

Income and Income Sources

A manager must know what makes money for the group and must also know *where* the money comes from. Most organizations have a variety of **income sources**. This manager (at Clark's Software) is busy determining how much income came in from each source during the last year.

Notice that Clark's Computer Training income exceeds its income from Software Sales; however, its Software Sales exceeds income from Customer Support. This type of information is easily accessible when financial statistics, as outlined in the Admin Scale, are properly tracked. If your finance area is currently unable to give you this type of information when you need it, reorganize things so that you can get it easily.

Producing income is one part of the finance game; properly handling expenses is the other. There are many expenses associated with each of the sub-products that go into the making of a business's VFPs. Intelligent spending is key to viability.

Incurring expenses intelligently includes:

- Always knowing where (and for what) the money is being spent.
- Spending money in order to make money.

A finance manager (or any other manager) who does not keenly understand the VFPs and sub-products of an organization will not intelligently allocate funds or supervise finances.

Bean Theory

Bean theory describes the concept of spending money (beans) to make money (more beans). The term *bean theory* comes from an example of farming beans. A farmer uses a handful of beans to grow an entire crop of beans. The resulting crop has far more value than the original handful. However, other beans are used in growing crops, such as labor, fertilizer and equipment. When the value of the beans that were spent is compared to the value of the beans that were produced, a good manager winds up with a profit.

One allocates beans to make more beans. One spends money to make money. That is all there is to Bean Theory finance. In fact, it is one of the most basic elements of organizational finance.

Financial management is an activity that must (a) seek to prevent an organization from spending more money than it makes and (b) set aside enough money from its income to care for the group if it gets into a condition where it needs to be salvaged.

An organization will always spend all it makes (and even try to spend more). Businesses seem to adjust their "need" to how much money is made; thus, only when a surplus is made part of the "need" by disguised expense can a surplus occur. Only then will it occur. It will not happen otherwise.

You can only attain a financial cushion in an organization by moving it out of reach so that it appears spent, then producing it when the group overspends or gets into trouble.

Non-Producing Areas of an Organization

One must finance only those activities which will yield a result. One must refuse to finance non-producing areas or activities.

It is all too common to find low-producing areas demanding monies (or subsidies). No worthwhile manager will give in to such demands because, if widespread, will lead to insolvency.

Even though **costing** can be a time consuming activity, it can and must be done.

Product Development Costing

System Analysis	$8,000
Product Design	$17,000
Programming	$31,600
Testing	$5,700
Documentation	$4,000
Installation	$3,250
Support	$2,000/year
Maintenance	$1,800/year
Equipment	$157,000
Premises	$60,000
Legal Fees	$5,000
	$295,350

Complete costing is a detailed listing of the costs of an area, activity or action. This includes premises, pay of personnel, estimates of legal fees and every other sub-product which must be acquired or performed in order to achieve the organization's VFP.

Costing and Pricing

When pricing goods or services, one must be certain to consider all the finance principles outlined thus far in this section. The relationship between costing and pricing has an enormous impact on the solvency and profitability of any group. There can be many reasons for assigning one price versus another to a product; but regardless of cost, price, competition or volume, the most senior economic rule is "income must be greater than outgo."

One never sees the money that *wasn't* made due to improper financial allocation.

It is a big mistake to handle finances by "saving money" which should have been used to make more money.

Don't do any marketing. We can't possibly afford it right now.

What!?

The true losses incurred by an organization's unwillingness to allocate funds for sales and promotion can be calculated by the difference between:

- the money it made, and
- the money it should have made (and didn't).

An Index of Success

Money is not the end product of a business activity.

I love this software!

**Clark Software's
True End Product**

Clark's Solvency

Income

Outgo

**Measure of a
Good Manager**

The VFP (highly functional, user-friendly software in the hands of paid & happy customers) is the true end product of Clark's Software Company. However, Clark's financial solvency (as represented by the improving statistics) is a primary index of the ability and success of its managers.

In summary, a working knowledge of the subject of finance is senior to (and more basic than) the subject of accounting. Accounting involves methods of recording and presenting financial information. Finance is the activity of intelligently managing money to get results.

Make all the money you can. Spend less than that. That's the simple ABC of financial control. So it gives you a tax problem. So what? Your accountants should be capable of avoiding tax problems. Whether you do or don't have money, you will always have a tax problem. The way to solve tax problems is to have money, not to be broke.

No matter how good your intentions are as a manager, you will not find the route to prosperity if you ignore the principles of finance and solvency.

Conditions

As we outlined earlier, a statistic can be defined for every important activity within your company. This is true whether you are responsible for answering phone calls, making sales or running the company. Every sub-product or VFP that is produced is important to the survival of the organization. *Production* statistics provide vital information which is needed in order to successfully increase results.

One must be able to properly recognize what **condition** an area is in based on its statistics. This is covered in the following section.

Statistics Represent the Condition of an Area

The *trend* of the statistic represents the *condition* of operation in that area, which is to say *how* that area is doing!

There are various conditions which represent the degree of production (or the extent of success) being achieved in any given area.

Here is the **scale of conditions**. Each condition represents a higher level of production (results) than the condition below it.

Thomas and I are going to bring up one of our clients, Al Jones. Al is going to help us illustrate the conditions by using some examples from his own business. Come on up, Al.

Scale of Conditions*

Power
Power Change
Affluence
Normal
Emergency
Danger
Non-Existence

*Note: The trends of each of the above conditions are illustrated and explained on the following pages. Read on...

The Automobile Repair Shop

Al owns a very successful auto repair shop over in Clover Junction. He is going to go over various situations within his shop involving each of the conditions.

I studied the subject of statistics for a little while in college, but until I read about the Hubbard management principles I was unaware of the very special techniques I could use to *increase* results throughout my shop. I wanted a larger client base. I also wanted to see the production of my personnel improve. To be perfectly honest, I came to Thomas with quite a list of things I wanted to handle!

The following pages contain scenes from Al's shop which demonstrate each one of the conditions.

"A few years ago my auto repair sales were doing ok but then the economy turned sour and my shop went downhill. My sales were very low week in and week out. I became ever so aware of the decrease when Thomas had me create and keep graphs of it. Here you see my shop in Non-Existence."

The area above has fallen apart. It is in a condition of **Non-Existence**.

Non-Existence Condition

Power

Power Change

Affluence

Normal

Emergency

Danger

Non-Existence

When an area doesn't produce any valuable final products (or is non-viable) it is in the **condition of Non-Existence**. It is labeled Non-Existence because it isn't producing (as if it didn't exist).

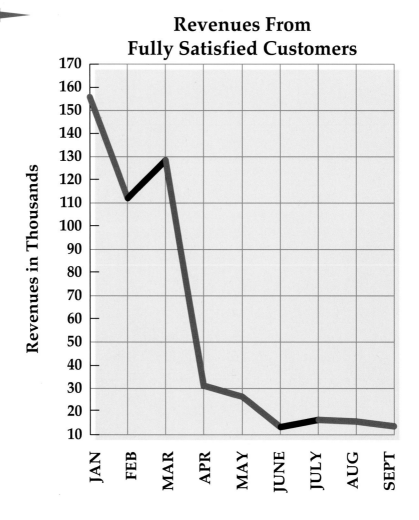

Revenues From Fully Satisfied Customers

As shown by the graph above, this area was once producing but is now no longer producing valuable results. It is in a condition of Non-Existence.

Power
Power Change
Affluence
Normal
Emergency
Danger
Non-Existence

If an employee has just come onto a new post or if an activity is just getting started (achieving no or limited results) a condition of Non-Existence will be present.

of Jobs Completed
(by new employee)

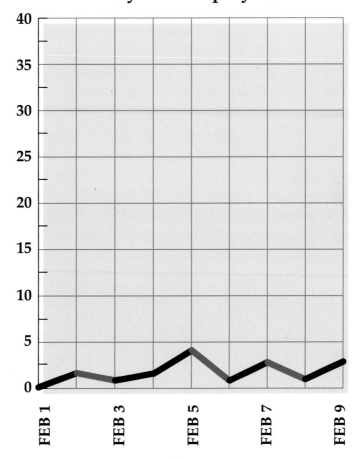

Non-Existence (as illustrated above and on the prior page) can come about in two ways:

- An activity just getting started (producing little, if any, results).

- An area that was once producing and is now failing to get results.

Both are referred to as Non-Existence.

Area in Danger

"I remember the day Thomas had me graph my solvency statistics (income vs. outgo). I realized that my shop as a whole was in Danger and no one (including myself) had been doing anything to handle it! We were all miserable because the money was so tight."

An area that is in **Danger** (such as the one above) must be handled *now*!

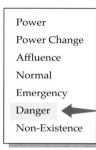

Power
Power Change
Affluence
Normal
Emergency
Danger
Non-Existence

A **Danger condition** exists when:

A. statistics show a continuing steady decline, or

B. a statistic plunges downward very steeply, or

C. a Senior Executive finds himself doing the job of another activity because that area is in trouble.

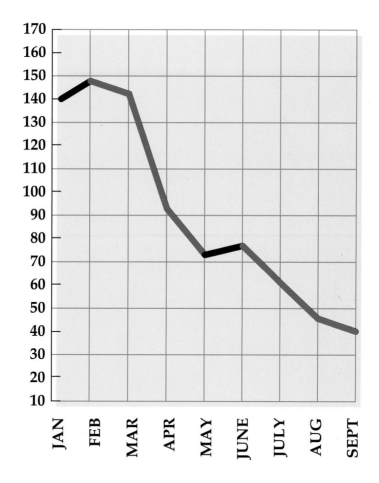

Any situation in Danger is dangerous because if the activity or area were to continue in a Danger condition it would simply cease to exist as a producing entity.

Area in Emergency

"There was a time when it seemed like we were getting fewer new customers than before. Then when I graphed the 'Number of New Customers' statistic, I was shocked to realize how right I was; we were in Emergency!"

If an area's statistics are in **Emergency**, you know that its production is not what it should be.

Emergency Condition

Power
Power Change
Affluence
Normal
Emergency
Danger
Non-Existence

An **Emergency condition** is represented by statistics that are unchanging or trending downward. When things are worsening they must be corrected. If the right actions are not taken then things can really fall apart.

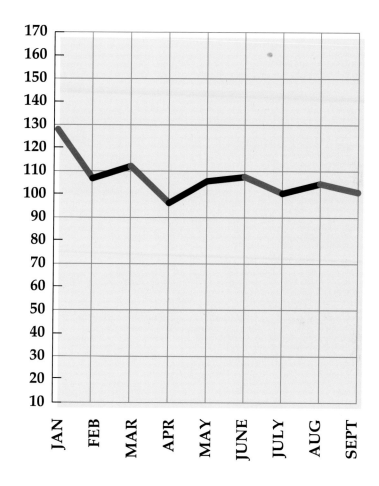

Things either expand or they contract. They do not remain level in this universe. Further, when something seeks to remain level and unchanged, it contracts. Therefore an unchanging statistic, as well as one that is worsening, are both in Emergency.

Area in Normal

"As I continued to learn about the conditions and exactly how to handle them, my shop started looking like I had intended it to! It was nice to watch my business getting stronger and stronger. Before long I had things under control."

There aren't many complaints about an area in **Normal** (one that is continually performing better and better).

Power

Power Change

Affluence

Normal

Emergency

Danger

Non-Existence

A **Normal condition** is represented by a routine or gradual increase in a statistic.

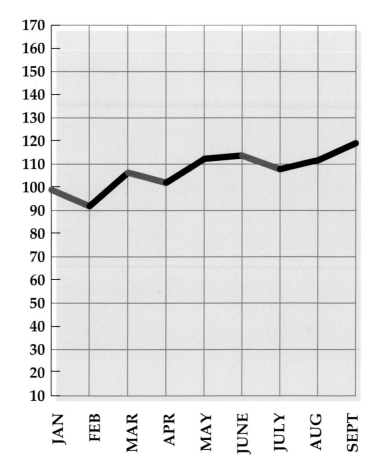

It is called Normal because things are running well. The results are neither stellar nor poor. They are steadily increasing which is good (normal).

Area in Affluence

"If I didn't track the stats, I wouldn't have been able to manage my shop so easily. I'm telling you, it's a miraculous technique. This scene shows the shop when things really got popping."

The above high producing area is in **Affluence**!

Affluence Condition

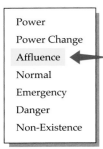

Power
Power Change
Affluence
Normal
Emergency
Danger
Non-Existence

An **Affluence condition** exists when there is a steep increase in a statistic (such as sudden peaks of income).

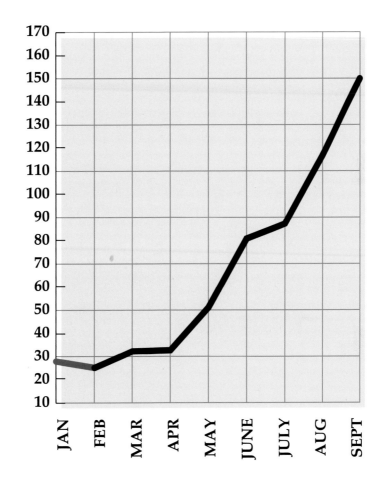

Things are obviously proceeding very well in those areas where Affluence conditions are present!

Area in Power

"When I first came to Thomas and Janet for some help, the idea of having my shop in a Power condition seemed like a far-off dream. But, after some studying and a lot of work, my dream became a reality.

There I am! Believe it or not, we handle a very high volume of auto repairs according to top quality standards every day. The customers are satisfied. My personnel are happy. And I love my work!

I strongly recommend the courses that Thomas and Janet, as well as other Hubbard consultants, offer. That's where you learn not only how to spot these conditions, but how to bring your business from any one of these conditions up into Power. And believe me that is where you want to be!!"

A **Power condition** is even better than Affluence.

Power
Power Change
Affluence
Normal
Emergency
Danger
Non-Existence

A Power condition is represented by a statistic that has gone into a very high range. It is a Normal trend in a brand-new range.

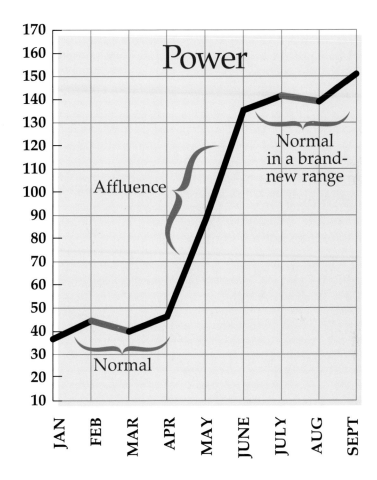

It is called Power because there is such an abundance of production that momentary halts or dips can not pull it down or imperil its survival.

Power Statistics Represent the Ideal Scene

No matter what the job or post may be, one should strive to attain Power conditions. One should expect this from one's associates as well.

It is the responsibility of every owner, manager and employee to ensure that the statistics in their area (and the organization as a whole) are on their way into Power.

Power
Power Change
Affluence
Normal
Emergency
Danger
Non-Existence

Let's discuss **Power Change**. Once you get an area truly into Power, you may want to turn it over to someone else. The following describes some important things you should know about the condition of Power Change.

There are only two circumstances which require replacement, the very successful one or the very unsuccessful one. Power Change involves the steps one would take when replacing another who had the post (or area) in a Power condition. Power Change ensures that the stellar results will continue.

When a staff member is promoted to a new position, the newcomer to that post will be inheriting a very successful "pair of boots." By correctly applying Power Change it is possible for a person to successfully "wear the boots" his predecessor left behind.

Many gifted individuals fail to significantly expand their organization or area because they don't apply the steps necessary to achieve Power or Power Change.

Improving Statistics

Now that you can easily recognize the conditions based on the trend of a statistic, it is imperative that you (as a manager, owner or employee) know how to successfully *improve* them.

Thank you very much, Al.

I want everyone here to know that Al spent valuable time in our courseroom studying the conditions and how to handle each of them. It was a pleasure to train him.

Mr. Hubbard's research on these conditions led to the discovery of an exact set of tools which, when used, can increase any and every statistic within your company. These tools are referred to as the **condition formulas**.

Each one of the conditions from Non-Existence through Power Change and Power has its own specific formula. Each formula is a precise conceptual outline of the steps that need to be taken in order to bring the area (to which the formula is being applied) into the next higher condition.

Power

Power Change

Affluence

Normal

Emergency

Danger

Non-Existence

The formula for each condition is listed in an exact sequence and the formula must be done in that sequence.

If the correct condition formula is fully and correctly applied, it will *always* result in improvement (that's the miracle of the formulas).

The following pages outline the detailed steps of *one* of the condition formulas (the Emergency formula).

The Emergency Formula

Here is the formula for an Emergency condition.

The Emergency Formula:

1. **Promote.**
   That applies to an organization. To an individual you had better say produce.
2. **Change your operating basis.**
3. **Economize.**
4. **Then prepare to deliver.**
5. **Stiffen discipline.**

If you were to complete the above steps on an area in Emergency, you would find that the area would move up into the next higher condition. In other words, immediately after steps 1 through 5 were honestly and fully completed, you would find that the area which was in Emergency is now in Normal. Let's look at each step in more detail.

Promote.

For an organization the first step of the Emergency Formula is **promote**.

Promotion can be done in many ways. It may mean advertise. Perhaps it means to go knock on doors. It could involve calling on the existing clients to ensure that they are happy. These are only a few of many ways one can promote.

Many organizations faced with down-trending statistics (Emergency) begin to cut advertising. This is *not* the right action. It may appear to save money, but it won't bring in the additional business necessary to revert the scene.

Emergency Step 1 (Produce)

Produce.

In the case of an individual, the first step of the Emergency Formula is **produce**.

This involves getting results regardless of what needs to be done. For an individual whose post is in Emergency (as indicated by the statistics on the job), step 1 of the Emergency Formula means, "Get on with it and produce!"

Change your operating basis.

The second step of the Emergency Formula (applying to both an organization and an individual) is **change your operating basis**.

You had better change your operating basis (meaning you can't just go about doing things the way you have been) because that operating basis led you or that activity into an Emergency. Otherwise (after promoting/producing) you wind up in another condition of Emergency.

Economize.

The third step of the formula is **economize**.

When the statistics start to recover, economize. Don't spend the fruits of the recent recovery... economize.

This could apply to a group's income as well as to an individual's time, speed or efficiency on the job.

Some people tend to keep themselves in a seemingly constant condition of Emergency because they do steps 1 and 2 (promote/produce and change their operating basis) but then they fail to economize. They spend everything they made. That doesn't work.

I'm sure you know of people who never even get past step 1 of the Emergency Formula. They promote or produce (step 1) when the stats go down, but then they don't do step 2 (change your operating basis), so they keep making the same mistakes over and over.

Such a person either doesn't know or doesn't apply the formula.

Prepare to deliver.

The fourth step is **prepare to deliver**. This involves whatever preparations are needed in order to deliver more products, results, etc. This may include organizing one's area or activities, purchasing or fixing any needed tools or possibly even getting one's questions answered (all in order to help ensure delivery occurs).

Whatever it is that needs to be done in order to make it more possible to deliver is completed during step 4 of the Emergency Formula.

Stiffen discipline.

The fifth step is **stiffen discipline**.

This could simply mean "not to go down to the pub every Friday night." Or, "Let's stiffen up the discipline, let's stay home and grind the midnight oil away." "Let's stay home and do some homework." "Let's be a little more regular on the job, work a little harder." "Let's not goof quite so much and make so many mistakes."

If discipline is not put in, life itself is going to discipline the individual, group or activity.

Power
Power Change
Affluence
Normal
Emergency
Danger
Non-Existence

Those are the five steps of the Emergency Formula and, if properly applied, they will bring one up into Normal; and if not they will send one down into Danger.

Power

Power Change

Affluence

Normal

Emergency

Danger

Non-Existence

If the condition of an area is Normal and the formula for a Normal condition is fully applied that area will move up into Affluence. Then (and only then), if the steps of the formula for an Affluence condition are applied, the area will go into Power. Again, one must keep in mind that this applies to *all* areas of an organization (Sales, Marketing, Finance or Production, etc.)

The Formulas are to be Applied

In order for an organization (or any of its areas) to survive well, the appropriate formula *must* be applied.

The statistics will not improve if:

- the wrong condition formula is applied,
- all the steps of the formula are not performed,
- the formula is misapplied.

Conditions below Non-Existence

There are also conditions *below* Non-Existence.

These lower conditions occur when a person or activity has not only ceased to be productive, but is knowingly or unknowingly diminishing the livelihood and well-being of others.

Power
Power Change
Affluence
Normal
Emergency
Danger
Non-Existence
Liability
Doubt
Enemy
Treason
Confusion

The lower conditions are described on the following pages.

The Condition of Confusion

This person is in a condition of **Confusion**. He isn't getting anything done.

When in a condition of Confusion the person or area will be in a state of random motion. There will be no real production, only disorder and confusion.

The Condition of Treason

Treason is defined as betrayal after trust.

Most business failures come about when trust is *mistakenly* placed in another person.

Although the waitress above was hired to provide excellent service (and was trusted to do so), she is actually driving away business, thus betraying the restaurant she is currently working for.

122

The Condition of Enemy

When a person is an avowed and knowing enemy of an individual, group, project or organization, a condition of **Enemy** exists.

...this is the third time this week one of my prospects did not receive the information you were supposed to send them.

So what! You're not my boss, you can't fire me, and besides, I don't care if you make those sales or not!

In the above example, the woman is clearly "not on the same team" as the salesman. She is actually stopping sales from occurring.

The Condition of Doubt

When one cannot make up one's mind as to an individual, group, organization or project, a condition of **Doubt** exists.

The man you see here is clearly having second thoughts about his teaching career. You can be sure he isn't doing his very best when it comes to teaching the students in front of him.

The Condition of Liability

Liability is assigned where careless or malicious and knowing damage is caused to projects, organizations or activities. It is adjudicated that it is malicious and knowing because orders have been published against it or because it is contrary to the intentions and actions of the remainder of the team or the purpose of the project or organization.

...well, I should go now Pete. I forgot to put the sign out again. But, before I go...

It is a liability to have such a person unwatched as the person may do or continue to do things to stop or impede the forward progress of the project or organization and such a person cannot be trusted.

Applying the Formulas

"While every condition has its own specific formula, only Emergency has been outlined in today's seminar. Our consulting firm (as well as many other Hubbard Management consulting firms around the world) offers comprehensive seminars, courses and workshops on the conditions and their formulas."

It is highly advisable for a manager to study and apply all the condition formulas and thus be able to correctly handle *any* management situation immediately.

The Formulas Yield Results

All of the condition formulas from Confusion through Power and Power Change yield exceptional results. Correct use of the conditions can dramatically improve one's life in areas where things have been progressing very poorly.

Up and Down the Conditions

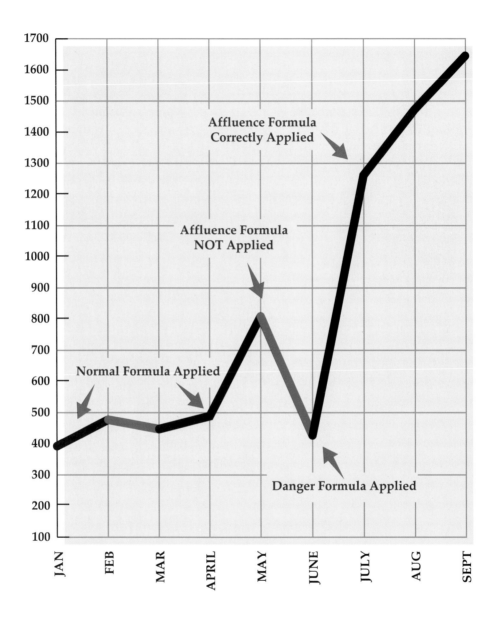

During the course of business it is common to find areas going from one condition to another. While it is the responsibility of all personnel to apply the appropriate condition to their post or area, a good manager can handle any area (using statistics and conditions) by ensuring that the correct formulas are applied.

Conditions are a Fact of Life

Conditions exist whether one is aware of them or not. They involve any and every activity in life (regardless of whether statistics are available for that activity).

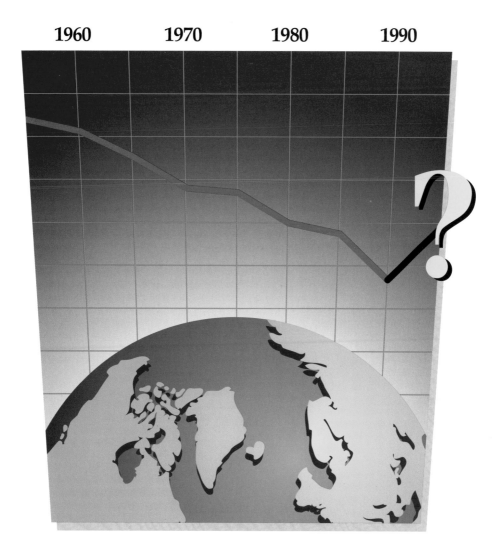

Conditions are basic to this universe. The size, scope or type of activity is irrelevant. You will find that when the correct formula is applied the scene will improve.

This book was written so that you would be more effective in improving conditions in your business, your life and on Earth in general.

Management by Statistics

There is a great deal more that can be done with statistics in addition to determining the conditions and applying their formulas. Once Al's shop was fully up and running on statistics (and conditions) he wanted to learn more about the powerful concepts of management by statistics.

The most direct observation in an organization (or a country) is statistics. These tell of production. They measure what is done. It cannot be said too often that management is best done by statistics.

Assigning Production Statistics

Every area and employee of an organization should be assigned production statistics which measure the results of the completed work.

Each employee must know and understand his duties (and statistics). They are then fully responsible and accountable for their results (which are shown in their statistics).

Comparing Statistics

One area of a group affects another which in turn affects others. Certain areas of a group may have an impact on *all* other areas within that group.

One can deduce a great deal about an organization by comparing the statistics of related areas.

Date Coincidence

When reviewing statistics one may notice dramatic changes in one or more of the graphs on a particular date. Obviously something caused the statistic to change. Once you isolate the date that the stats changed, you start asking questions about what might have changed at that time. The change in the business = the change in the statistics = the date both changes occurred = **date coincidence**.

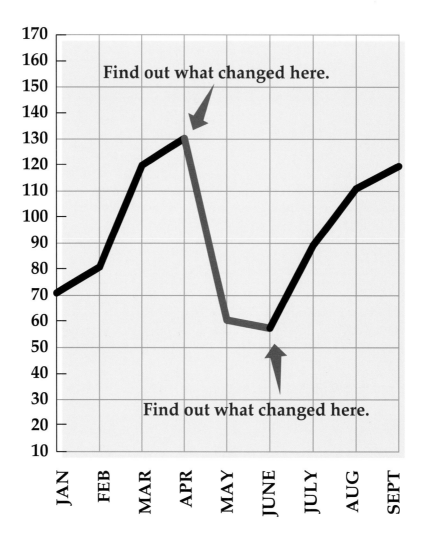

It would be difficult to isolate a date coincidence if you didn't have statistics for all areas. When you track statistical data the deduction process becomes relatively easy.

Statistics and Levels of Management

Higher levels of management are responsible for broader zones of production. The specific statistics used by upper management must reflect this.

Also note that lower level managers must manage by week to week changes in a condition's trend, whereas higher level managers must manage based on trends which span longer periods of time.

Collecting the Correct Stats

By now you should have a crisp new perspective on the value of sensible statistics. We have seen that they are an integral part of the Admin Scale. Over time, they represent the level of exchange of a group where *Exchange in Abundance* is the highest.

Statistics provide key information which leads to intelligent use of Bean Theory (spending money to make money). Plus, the entire scale of conditions from Non-Existence through Power is determined from them. Good statistics open the door to many additional uses.

The powerful technique of managing by statistics works *only* if:

- the statistics are collected (always and without fail),
- the statistics which are reported are accurate,
- the appropriate statistics are tracked for each area.

Leadership

We've reviewed the science of management by statistics; now we're going to move into the subject of managing people.

Although it is commonly believed that leadership ability is something that one must be born with, it is important to realize that it is something that can be taught, cultivated, developed and strengthened.

One of our clients, Peter Dodgeston of Standard Automobile & Motor Company, came to us because he wanted to gain the abilities necessary to effectively motivate his employees. He wanted to expand his company and knew that it would only be possible if his staff was operating as a true team, striving for the same goals.

Thomas and I will be using examples from Peter's company to demonstrate certain leadership qualities.

Learning how to become more effective as an executive, manager, captain, etc. comes from understanding the fundamentals of leadership itself.

Goal Finder / Founder

Every group has (or had) a goal finder, goal setter or dream maker. This is most commonly its founder. A group always starts with a vision. No matter how bad things get, the true goals of a group remain as pure and as far-reaching as the very first time they were dreamt. This is rarely understood and yet it is the single most powerful truth behind any group.

In a large group the goal finder often is not the management. It is not the responsibility of management to "know better" than the goal finder. It is their charter to help make the original dream a reality.

True *leadership* is found in those who can keep the goals and purposes alive in every member of the group. This applies to management as well as to the goal finder.

"We sat down with Peter and drew up a comprehensive Admin Scale for his company. When this was done the weak points in his organization became very apparent."

A precise definition of management is: *The skill with which goals, purposes, policy, plans, programmes, projects, orders, ideal scenes, statistics and valuable final products in any activity are aligned and gotten into action.*

Managers Implement Policy

Once Peter had a set of workable policies which aligned with the goals, he knew it was his job to put them into effect.

A strong manager both follows and enforces the policies of the group. A weak manager does neither.

The essence of good management is caring what goes on.

A good manager cares what happens, what's spent, what prosperity can occur, how the work is done, how the place looks, how the staff really fares. He is dedicated to getting the show on the road and he takes out of the lineup obstacles to the organization's (and staff's) progress.

Caring what goes on and not caring is the basic difference.

Getting Products (Results)

"Caring" and "being nice" are not necessarily the same thing. For example, if a "nice" manager accepts the reasons given for non-production without handling and correcting it, then despite the arguments some persons might raise, that manager doesn't really care about the customers, the operation, or its personnel.

A manager is there to ensure that results occur. He *may* or *may not* be nice about it. However, despite anything, if he is a manager at all, his area will get results.

Half-Dones, Not-Dones and Backlogs

Half-dones and not-dones lead to backlogs. When confronted with an area with lots of tasks that are half-done or not-done a manager should beware.

Backlogs are a strong indicator that something is very wrong with the production in that area.

Do What you're Doing While you're Doing it.

Some employees have their mind on something other than what they are doing. Regardless of what is said, they are less effective than they would be if they paid attention to their work.

The rule to efficient and effective production is "Do what you're doing while you're doing it."

It is the responsibility of a manager to see that those things in his areas which are started get completed. Incomplete actions do not result in VFPs, they cannot be exchanged; yet they cost resources and thus deplete the organization's wherewithal. When a product is gotten it is a "done." The key word here is *done*. Get real "dones" and the operation works smoothly.

Overloading an Area

It is important to note that you should not assign someone so many tasks (at the same time) that they can never finish any of them.

As the unhandled work piles up the statistics of overloaded areas will dive, crashing the statistics of related areas as well.

How to Handle Work

When faced with a tremendous number of incomplete tasks (backlogs), the trick is to take one and do it. Get it done. Get it completely done. Then take on another (one at a time). You'll soon find that you are on top of it all. The key to handling work is to *do it now*.

One would, of course, use common sense to determine which tasks to handle first. Also, one would *not* drop out the regular day-to-day responsibilities while handling the backlogs.

Targets

A target is an objective one intends to accomplish in a given period of time. Setting targets is part of the bread and butter of managing.

A target is a tangible, realizable aim. The manager points to the target, and the group meets it.

A quota is the number assigned to whatever is to be produced. It is a future expectancy.

Too low a quota

Nearly impossible challenge

Too impossible

Quota: 1 contract completed

Quota: 10 contracts completed

Quota: 50 contracts completed

The way one sets a quota is quite important. If the quota is too impossible to meet then you wind up with overwhelmed personnel and no results. If the quota is nearly impossible it quite often gets made as it is a challenge. Too low a quota is no challenge at all and yields lesser results.

Intention

Accomplishing a target or a quota requires *intention*. Intention is the idea that one is going to accomplish something. If you intend something to happen, it happens.

Strong leadership requires intention.

Note: Verbalization is not the intention. The intention is the carrier wave which takes the verbalization along with it.

There is a certain spirit or degree of liveliness (or lack of it) which exists in any team, business or group. It comes from the morale of its individuals. This factor of morale is basic to any group.

Any leader/manager needs to know the following rule: *Production is the basis of morale.* A group's air of confidence is based on the results that are being produced by each individual *and* by the group as a whole.

Contribution, Commendation and Acknowledgement

Every employee or member of the group is there to contribute ideas or efforts to the team. It is important to acknowledge contributions.

Approval and commendation are often far more valuable than material rewards and are usually worked for far harder than mere pay.

Commendations, bonuses and promotions must be based on production (not office politics). Basing them on anything else is detrimental to the team.

When you reward down statistics and penalize up statistics you get down statistics. If you reward nonproduction you get nonproduction. When you penalize production you get nonproduction.

These principles apply to raises, bonuses and promotions as well as verbal acknowledgements or written commendations. Never promote a down statistic or demote an up statistic.

Note: The concept above is vital to a family, a business, or any government.

Anyone will discover in actually dealing with people that these factors dominate:

1. People are willing to do their best and will until hammered about it.

2. Most causes for complaint are based not on misconduct but on misunderstanding.

3. Only personal contact can restore understanding.

4. Written criticism or anger is rarely repaired by more writing. A breach opened by writing is usually susceptible to being healed only by personal contact. The moral is, therefore, don't open the breach with a distempered dispatch.

5. Don't let a detected error drift. Take it up and correct it when found.

6. Don't accumulate "bad marks" against personnel before acting. Forget old "bad marks" when they have been corrected.

7. A person has his side of the story. As the one on the job he has more valid data than the executive. Listen and question before you decide you are outraged.

8. The only capital an executive has is the willingness *to work*. Preserve it. No person can be driven to labor– as every slave society has found out. They always lose. When a man is whipped, that work he then does still stems from his willingness alone. Anger made it smaller.

Hats

The vast majority of today's business professionals grossly underestimate the extent to which excellent training solves most organizational woes. Any good manager prefers harmony within the group, but more importantly, a manager seeks results. Where there are no results there will be no group. This all ties together in a very simple fashion– if you want results from your team members, they've got to be adequately trained in the know-how of what it takes to get the kind of results you seek!

Low-quality training accomplishes nothing. In fact it often sets the individual (and the group) back. It's harder to train them later because they now think they already know. An example of this is the various MBA programs which teach management principles that are confusing, incomplete and either far too complex for real life or fundamentally unsound.

The solution to all this is to train managers on management principles that work.

The Hampton Lee Production Company

In addition to his expertise in management, Mr. Hubbard had extensive experience educating people. He did a great deal of research regarding both the old-school and modern practices used in business and education. He threw out the techniques that didn't work and developed additional administrative treasures necessary to gain a complete understanding of the subject.

One of our clients, Hampton Lee, owns a television commercial production company. Mr. Lee came to us with personnel problems that were causing his profits to go down the drain. The amount of money that can be lost on a poorly run set is astronomical! He knew that if he could get others to perform their jobs well, he would make money hand over fist.

Scenes from the Hampton Lee Production Company are used in the following pages to describe the concepts of hats & hatting.

A **hat** is the duty or duties of a certain post. The term *hat* originated from the fact that posts are often distinguished by the type of hat worn. *Hatting* is the action done to train someone on the duties of his post/hat.

Policeman

Chef

Actor!

Fireman

When people are doing their jobs as expected they are said to be "wearing their hats." Likewise, if people are not providing what is needed and wanted they are "not wearing their hats."

#1 Source of Problems

If statistics are down, it usually traces back to someone's deficiency in knowledge or understanding of his basic job/post responsibilities. This particular personnel problem is extremely basic; however, it is also very common.

The director has just realized that this actor is confused about who is actually responsible for what.

When someone truly understands his or her hat they can easily and accurately provide the expected results of their post.

Hats and Products

Every hat in an organization has its own product. The person wearing the hat is responsible for its results.

As covered earlier, statistics measure the results of any given post (or hat) in an organization. The condition of those statistics shows you how well that individual is wearing his hat.

Hat Write-Ups

A **hat write-up** is a complete summary of the exact duties of a particular post.

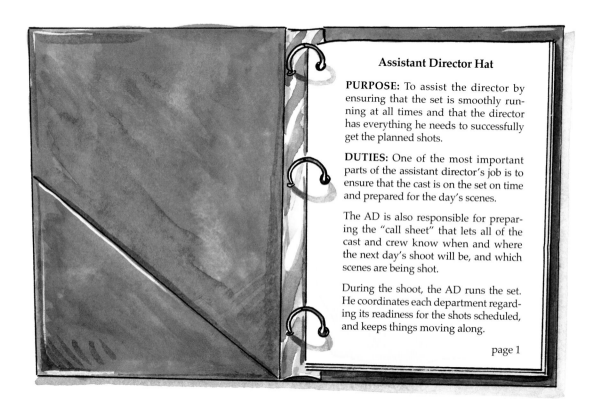

> **Assistant Director Hat**
>
> **PURPOSE:** To assist the director by ensuring that the set is smoothly running at all times and that the director has everything he needs to successfully get the planned shots.
>
> **DUTIES:** One of the most important parts of the assistant director's job is to ensure that the cast is on the set on time and prepared for the day's scenes.
>
> The AD is also responsible for preparing the "call sheet" that lets all of the cast and crew know when and where the next day's shoot will be, and which scenes are being shot.
>
> During the shoot, the AD runs the set. He coordinates each department regarding its readiness for the shots scheduled, and keeps things moving along.
>
> page 1

A hat write-up includes such information as the purpose of the job and a description of the products for that area as well as the statistic(s) for the job. The use of hat write-ups greatly expedites the training of any new or transferred employee.

A large part of a manager's hat is to make certain that others wear their hats. A manager needs to get the hatting material into the hands of the employees (in this case, the shooting crew) then ensure that they know its content. In time, this makes the manager's job a breeze.

A good manager knows that the staff must understand and apply the information contained in the hat write-ups.

Understanding Others' Hats

It is imperative that one first knows and understands his or her own hat. However, in order to work as a team it is important to be very familiar with the hats worn by others.

In fact, the strongest executives are those who truly understand each hat worn by anyone in the group.

Hats and Hat Write-Ups

When every team member becomes expert at his or her hat, an enormous amount of high-quality work can be accomplished in a short period of time.

"By the way, Mr. Lee isn't here in today's seminar audience. He wrapped up his recent shoots, gave his staff bonuses, deposited the extra money in his newly opened Swiss bank account and is now vacationing in the Caribbean."

Hats are Invaluable

The proper use of hats and hatting preserves valuable know-how in a group. It all too often occurs that "the new broom sweeps clean," referring to an individual new to a post who wipes out all the policies and standards being used by that post's predecessor. This practice is generally very detrimental. Bad policies, when found, of course need to be changed. But when good policies get knocked out, a group or one of its areas can fall fast and hard.

Entire professions, industries and even civilizations have collapsed because they ignored this point. Hats and hatting are vitally important to any and every group. This is something a manager must *never* forget.

The Organizing Board

Breakthroughs regarding the use of hats & hatting led Mr. Hubbard to another exceptional management tool. It is called the **organizing board** or **org board** for short. We will use Clark Software's org board as an example.

Hats and posts must be coordinated within an organization in order to achieve maximum efficiency and results.

The org board is used to actively organize and control the flows of communication, command and production in a business.

Sample Org Board

"Here is a basic outline of an org board. It has seven divisions and twenty-one departments."

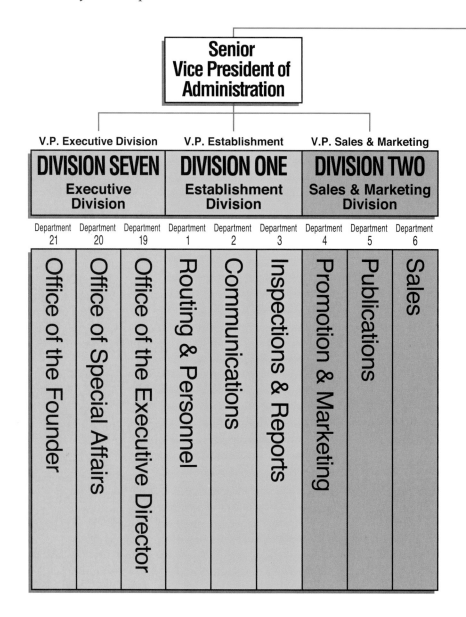

Although the organizing board seems to have a great many departments, and would fit only a large group, it fits any organization of any size. A group, if it is to survive, must ensure that each hat is worn as represented by the divisions and departments of the org board.

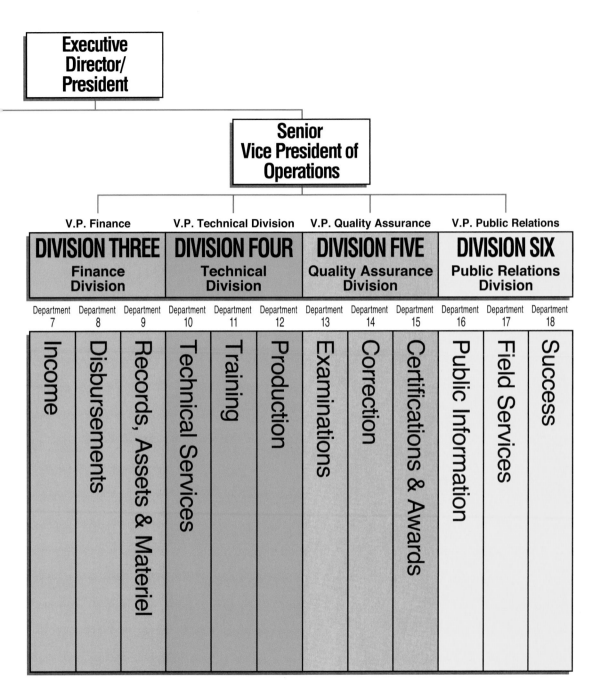

	Executive Director/ President			

	Senior Vice President of Operations			

V.P. Finance	V.P. Technical Division	V.P. Quality Assurance	V.P. Public Relations
DIVISION THREE Finance Division	**DIVISION FOUR** Technical Division	**DIVISION FIVE** Quality Assurance Division	**DIVISION SIX** Public Relations Division

Department 7	Department 8	Department 9	Department 10	Department 11	Department 12	Department 13	Department 14	Department 15	Department 16	Department 17	Department 18
Income	Disbursements	Records, Assets & Materiel	Technical Services	Training	Production	Examinations	Correction	Certifications & Awards	Public Information	Field Services	Success

When you look at the division names you can see what is missing in your own activities. By studying this you can see why businesses fail. They lack one or another of these divisions. No matter how organized any company, society, or political entity is, it may be as unsuccessful as it has these functions missing.

Chain of Command

The chain of command in any group must flow from the top down.

While an org board outlines the command structure, it is not simply a command chart or flow chart. It is actually a highly advanced organizational tool.

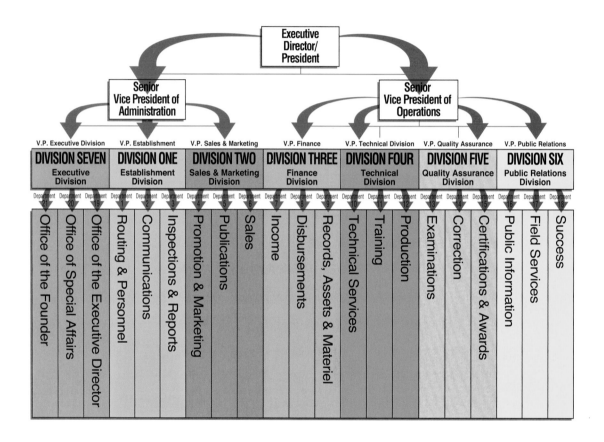

A good org board, well grooved in, with duties well apportioned permits things to smooth out and increase in volume without strain. In a flood if you can channel the water, you can handle the flood. If you just batter at water you drown. Organizational genius is composed only of arranging sequences of action and designating channels for types of particles. That's all it is.

Communication Lines and Channels

An org board has built-in paths of communication lines and channels.

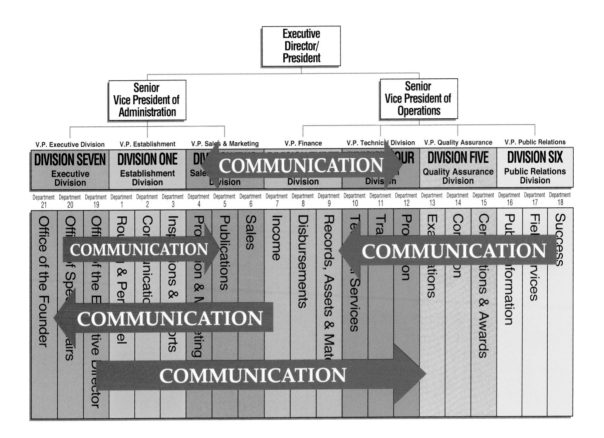

The *normal* flow of communication in an organization is horizontal, from one employee to another. The only communication that needs to go up the command channel (involving seniors) are permissions, authorizations, information, important actions or compliance. Communications involving orders are sent down the org board's command channels (from seniors to juniors).

Flat Org Charts

You will find many small businesses where everyone (incorrectly) reports to one person. Such a "flat-line org chart" is not an org board. When this is the case, the one in charge gets exhausted; and despite endless hours of hard work, such a business will not grow.

When a senior executive runs a large business as if it had a flat org chart the results are disastrous.

Divisions, Departments, Sections and Units

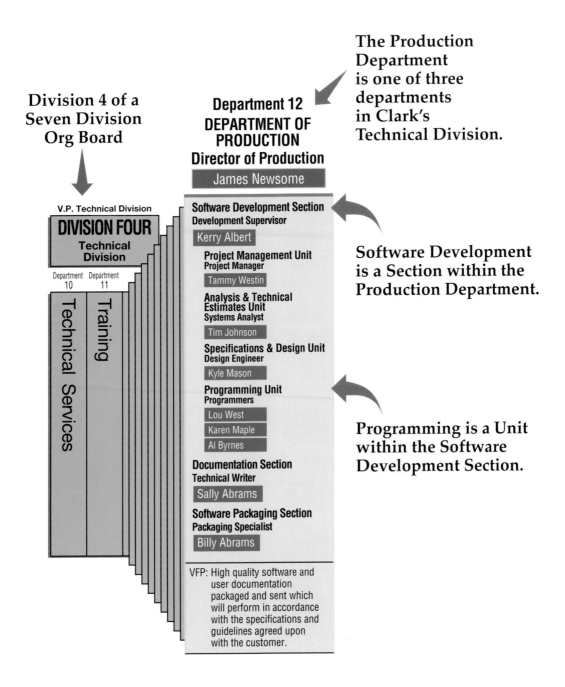

Division 4 of a
Seven Division
Org Board

Department 12
DEPARTMENT OF PRODUCTION
Director of Production

James Newsome

The Production
Department
is one of three
departments
in Clark's
Technical Division.

V.P. Technical Division

DIVISION FOUR
Technical Division

Department 10   Department 11

Technical Services

Training

Software Development Section
Development Supervisor

Kerry Albert

Software Development
is a Section within the
Production Department.

Project Management Unit
Project Manager

Tammy Westin

Analysis & Technical Estimates Unit
Systems Analyst

Tim Johnson

Specifications & Design Unit
Design Engineer

Kyle Mason

Programming Unit
Programmers

Lou West

Karen Maple

Al Byrnes

Programming is a Unit
within the Software
Development Section.

Documentation Section
Technical Writer

Sally Abrams

Software Packaging Section
Packaging Specialist

Billy Abrams

VFP: High quality software and user documentation packaged and sent which will perform in accordance with the specifications and guidelines agreed upon with the customer.

An org board is grouped into divisions which are made up of departments which in turn are further broken down into sections and units.

Org Board, Hats and Products

An org board is organized by major function (activities or responsibilities).

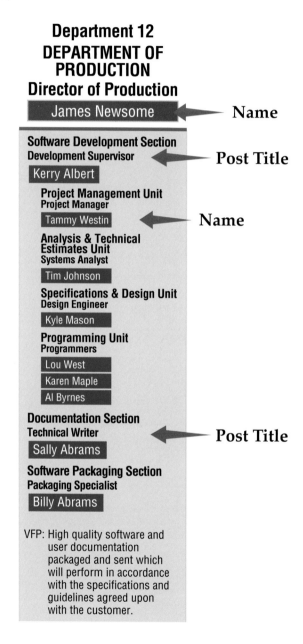

The org board must contain every post that exists within the organization, including the names of the personnel who are responsible for them.

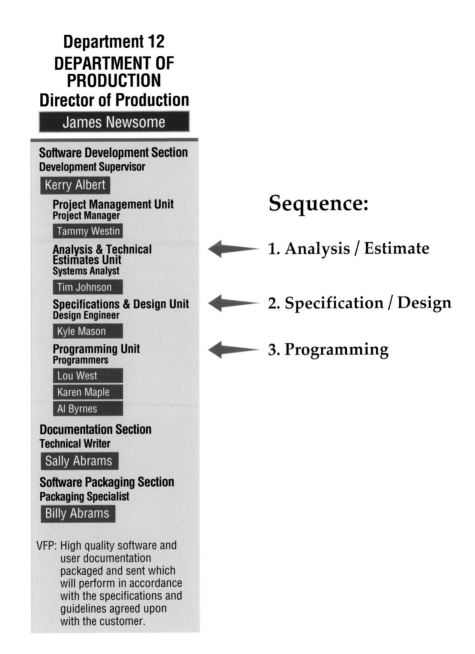

Department 12
DEPARTMENT OF PRODUCTION
Director of Production

James Newsome

Software Development Section
Development Supervisor

Kerry Albert

Project Management Unit
Project Manager

Tammy Westin

Analysis & Technical Estimates Unit
Systems Analyst

Tim Johnson

Specifications & Design Unit
Design Engineer

Kyle Mason

Programming Unit
Programmers

Lou West

Karen Maple

Al Byrnes

Documentation Section
Technical Writer

Sally Abrams

Software Packaging Section
Packaging Specialist

Billy Abrams

VFP: High quality software and user documentation packaged and sent which will perform in accordance with the specifications and guidelines agreed upon with the customer.

Sequence:

1. Analysis / Estimate

2. Specification / Design

3. Programming

Also built into the org board is the correct sequence of activities (sub-products) that result in the VFPs of the organization. For example, at Clark's Software an Analysis and Estimate is done before the Design and Specification which is then followed by Programming.

Sub-Products in Sequence

1. Analysis / Estimate

2. Specification / Design

3. Programming

The org board shows what functions are done in the organization, the order in which they are done and who is responsible for them.

Each division, department, etc. has a VFP accompanied by one or more production statistics. It will be found that every portion (large or small) of the org board has a product or products (VFPs) for which that area is responsible.

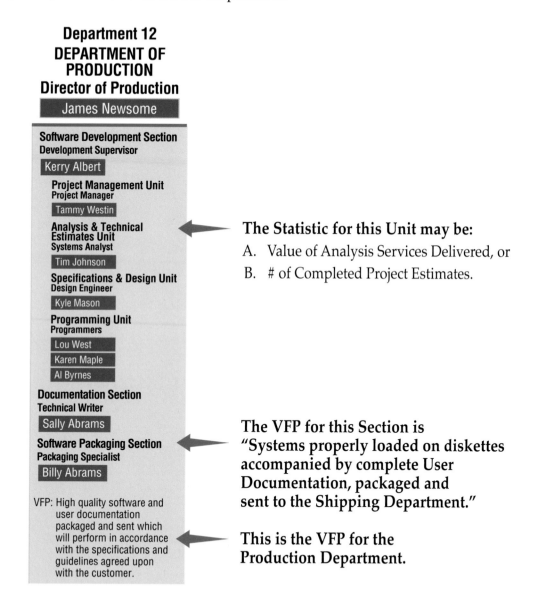

Department 12
DEPARTMENT OF PRODUCTION
Director of Production
James Newsome

Software Development Section
Development Supervisor
Kerry Albert

Project Management Unit
Project Manager
Tammy Westin

Analysis & Technical Estimates Unit
Systems Analyst
Tim Johnson

Specifications & Design Unit
Design Engineer
Kyle Mason

Programming Unit
Programmers
Lou West
Karen Maple
Al Byrnes

Documentation Section
Technical Writer
Sally Abrams

Software Packaging Section
Packaging Specialist
Billy Abrams

VFP: High quality software and user documentation packaged and sent which will perform in accordance with the specifications and guidelines agreed upon with the customer.

The Statistic for this Unit may be:

A. Value of Analysis Services Delivered, or

B. # of Completed Project Estimates.

The VFP for this Section is "Systems properly loaded on diskettes accompanied by complete User Documentation, packaged and sent to the Shipping Department."

This is the VFP for the Production Department.

The combined products of each department result in the VFPs for the division. The cumulative VFPs of all the divisions represent the overall VFP of the group as a whole. Each area of the organization must be on the org board and must have a statistic.

Any Size of Group

The conceptual guidelines of org boarding apply to any group regardless of its size or its product. It goes from one person to thousands without change.

Org Boards Assist in Managing by Statistics

An org board reduces confusion. It tells everyone what to expect from everyone else. If anyone in the group has a question about lines, channels, command hierarchy, products, hats, zones of responsibility or the like, they will get an instant orientation by looking at the org board.

Where production sequences are not well-defined you will find many outpoints, such as one person reporting to two seniors, or you may find that no one thinks they are responsible for certain functions which are, in fact, quite vital to the group.

In order to analyze statistics one must have the correct statistics available. The org board helps to establish a foundation from which a group can more easily implement management by statistics for all its areas.

Organizational Communication

Clean Horizons and Communication

We are now going to dive straight into the subject of communication. We will be addressing this subject with the help of Clean Horizons, the environmental firm we used to illustrate the concepts of the Admin Scale. There is quite a bit to know about the subject of communication; however, we will only be touching upon its basics today.

Communication is one of the most fundamental activities in life, yet is often the source of much confusion in organized activities.

Note: There are many courses available from Hubbard Colleges and Hubbard Consultants around the world which focus on improving communication in business.

Communication

Communication can be defined as the interchange of ideas between people.

Organizations have a tremendous amount of communication occurring every day, whether written or spoken. Without communication any activity would simply cease to exist.

While the org board outlines the structure of a group, communication is the lifeline of any organized activity.

The Formula of Communication

In order to effectively communicate, one must first understand the component parts of communication.

The **formula of communication** is: Cause, Distance, Effect, with Intention, Attention and Duplication* WITH UNDERSTANDING. This formula is illustrated in the following pages.

* Duplication is the action of reproducing something exactly. Duplication precedes understanding.

Cause, Distance, Effect with Intention and Attention

The person who originates the communication is the **cause point**. The communication travels a **distance** to reach its destination which is the receipt or **effect point**.

Intention

Attention

Distance

CAUSE POINT

EFFECT POINT

For any communication to occur there must also be **intention** (the desire to cause the communication to reach its recipient) and **attention**, as illustrated above.

Duplication with Understanding

With the presence of these factors: *cause point*, *distance*, *effect point*, *intention* and *attention*, a message can then be delivered, **duplicated** and **understood**.

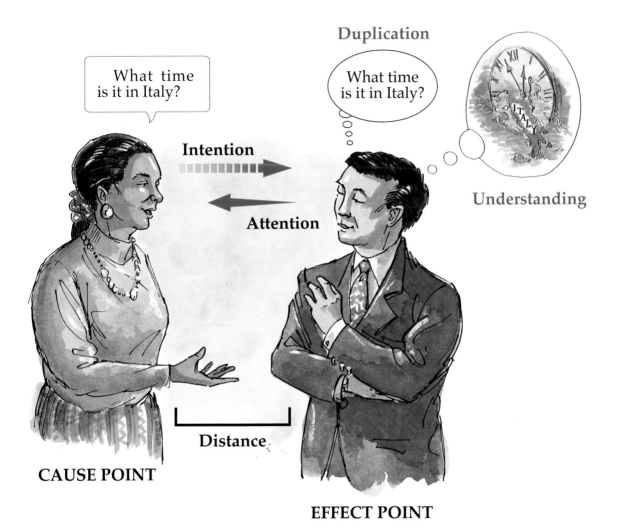

Duplication *precedes* understanding. One has to first duplicate (copy exactly) the communication before it can be understood. For example, if the communication is delivered, but not heard at the effect point, it cannot be duplicated as it was not heard and will not be understood.

The Complete Cycle

Once the communication formula is completed and the effect point has understood the communication, it now reverses where the cause point and effect point switch roles. The person who had received the communication may now become the originator (the cause point) of a new communication (the answer, the acknowledgement, response, etc.).

Only when each step has been completed has a true **communication cycle** taken place.

The Communication Formula Must be Complete

The communication formula is fundamental and true for *any* communication. If any part of the communication formula is not present you can expect problems.

For example, let's take just one part of the formula out and see what happens...

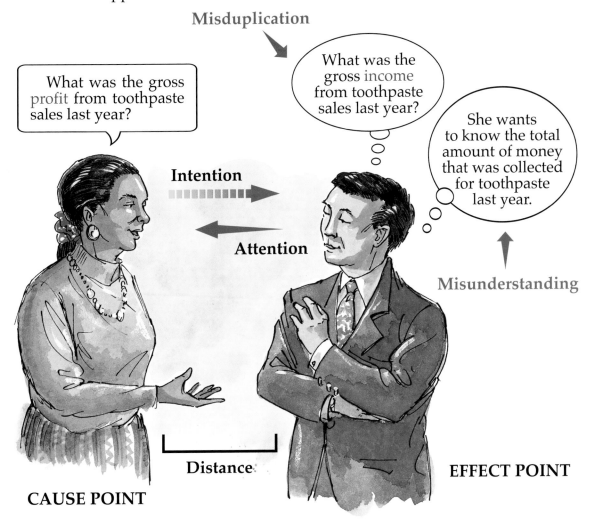

Abbey *(cause point)* wants *(intention)* to ask Steve *(effect point)* a question. Abbey sees that Steve is listening *(attention)* and asks him the question. The question travels to Steve *(distance)*, he hears what was asked but doesn't duplicate it. Thus Steve will not have an understanding of the communication that was just delivered. Steve will of course act upon the communication incorrectly.

Understanding

Understanding results in action.

It is lunacy to expect someone to do (or produce) something they did not understand. This concept applies to the giving of orders as well as to the duties of an entire post.

It is the responsibility of everyone in the group (owner, manager, employee, etc.) to ensure that they deliver *and* receive communications that are easily understood.

Speed of Communication

Communications within a group must not only be clear, they must also move swiftly.

There is an important rule regarding this; *speed of particle flow alone determines power.*

Speed applies to each aspect of a group's communications (such as letters, dispatches, faxes, products and even people's bodies). When a communication is received and understood, action should result. Putting responses off "until tomorrow" is needless when they can and should be done now.

Speed and Quality of Communication

When applying the rule of speed to communications the fundamental communication formula must never be violated. Speed must not degrade the actual quality of communication. One must not focus on speed alone as it could actually create misduplicated and misunderstood communications.

In summary, an increase in the speed and quality of communication is alone sufficient to greatly improve relations in any friendship, family, group or nation.

Developed Traffic

Traffic

The daily activities of any normal business such as messages, communications, people, paperwork, motion and the like are referred to as **traffic**.

Traffic

Traffic

Traffic

Traffic

Traffic

Ideally the traffic runs smoothly day in and day out.

Developed Traffic (Dev-T)

Most organizations have a *huge* amount of confused and unnecessary traffic. This burdens both production and communication lines. It is referred to as **developed traffic** or **dev-t**. It is created (developed), inapplicable, unhandled work (traffic). It is referred to as developed traffic because it develops more work unnecessarily for anyone involved.

"Developed" traffic does *not* mean usual and necessary traffic. It means *unusual and unnecessary traffic.*

Request for Supplies

The word *dev-t* has been coined because no other word exists which fits the true concept of what it means. The concept covers certain phrases like "why was this sent to me?" or "what is he doing that for?" or "this has no value!" or "this is ridiculous!" or "why all this double work?" or "why bother me with that?", etc. The term **dev-t** describes these and many others.

Dev-T Destroys Production

Mis-routing communications within a group or assigning tasks incorrectly serves to slow everything down. Additional traffic is then required to either get things put on the right channels or assigned to the correct post.

This is also true in reverse. When people handle work that is not associated with their post, they are creating additional traffic. They had to stop wearing their own hat in order to wear someone else's! These are all examples of dev-t.

Dev-t can destroy any real production in an organization while making it seem frantically busy.

Dev-T and Unhattedness

The cause of dev-t is *unhattedness*.

People who do not know what they are supposed to do or produce will take on traffic that does not belong to them, originate traffic they have no business with and send traffic to wrong persons or posts who don't handle it. Not knowing their own posts, they refer things they should handle to others who don't handle them either. Thus, the organization loads up with not-dones, half-dones, and backlogs.

Dropped Hats and Hat Dumping

When someone does not perform the duties he or she is responsible for, it is called a **dropped hat** or a **hat dump**. This is a major form of dev-t.

The real solution to dev-t is well-trained staff and managers who see that hats are being worn.

Musical Chairs

Musical chairs describes the continual transfer and re-posting of personnel. It creates widespread dev-t. A manager who allows this can destroy his organization.

It takes a while to train someone on a post and get the post in order. So rapid transfers defeat any post training or competence. The problem solved by the transfer creates another one in the area from which the person was transferred.

Strong communication lines, a well done org board and extensive training are each required in order for a group to eliminate dev-t and realize its potential.

Strong hatting and org boarding exposes sources of dev-t. It is the manager's responsibility to get the lines in place and then to see that they are used.

Far too many groups run on a **"hey-you" org board** where the manager doesn't actually follow the lines or the hats outlined on the org board. In such a group, the manager sees someone and says "hey you over there, do this..."instead of telling the correct person (to whom the hat belongs) to do it.

Note: A department head must never begin a practice of yanking people off post to do things that aren't a part of their hat. This is the most common executive failure because it puts confusion into the department. Yanking people off post makes them feel insecure. They get the idea they're partly fired and they quit, strange as it seems.

A manager's best solutions are hatting and stringent use of the org board. An unhatted organization is a madhouse to work in as no one knows what he's supposed to handle or what others should do. They don't go idle. They introduce Sahara sandstorms of dev-t.

An unhatted organization is also a lazy organization and *refers* everything to someone else.

A person who is hatted can control his post. When a person is uncertain, he cannot control his post. He cannot control his position. He feels weak. He goes slow. If he can control his post and its actions he feels competent. He can work effectively and rapidly.

The basic law is:

HATTING = CONTROL.

Personnel Training Programmes

Complete hatting does not occur overnight. It is done on a gradient. Every employee should always have a training programme which outlines the training needed for their current post. This should also eventually include the training necessary for the post to which they will be promoted.

An individually-tailored training programme establishes a useful and organized flow of personnel enhancement. Depending upon the organization, the training may be delivered internally, externally or both.

**Clean Horizons
Public Relations Personnel
Training Programme**

1. Clean Horizons' Orientation Pack
2. How to Achieve Effective Learning Course
3. Improving Business Through Communications Course
4. Formulas For Business Success Course
5. Study the Public Relations Hat Write-Ups
6. Management By Statistics Course
7. Listen to the How to Evaluate and Predict Human Behavior Lectures
8. Public Relations Course

If you and your associates take the time to study the Hubbard management principles on hatting, org boards, communication, and dev-t (and really understand them), you will notice a great reduction in the confusions of your everyday business activities accompanied by a significant increase in the group's productivity.

Seminar Summary

So, in the end, what is organization?

The essence of organization is:

- org boarding,

- the use of good judgement in assigning personnel to posts,

- plus training and hatting regarding the duties that each person is to perform.

In addition to this, the personnel must actually perform the duties so that the activity is productive.

Another ingredient that goes hand in hand with organization and survival is toughness. The ability to stand up, confront and handle whatever comes the way of the organization depends utterly on the ability of the individuals of the organization to stand up to, confront and handle what comes the individual's way. The composite whole of this ability makes a tough organization.

Confidence in one's teammates is another factor in organization survival. Confidence in one's self is something that has to be earned. It is respect.

A well-organized group survives. It is a team effort. But a team doesn't perform well if it doesn't know the right tools to use and the way to best use them. This seminar was intended to introduce you and your group to some outstanding management and organizational tools.

We've covered many areas today and I want to thank you for coming. I hope you enjoyed the seminar and found the information useful.

Janet and I would also like to extend a special acknowledgement to the executives and staff of Clean Horizons, Christopher's Golden Nugget, Clark's Software, Clover Junction Auto Repair, Standard Automobile & Motor Company and the Hampton Lee Production Company for their participation in the seminar.

The floor is now open for questions.

There were many questions.

Thanks Thomas and Janet!

Most of the attendees wanted individual help for their businesses. Thomas and Janet completed the seminar, but their work as consultants had just begun. We appreciate their time and input!

Wrapping it Up

The Principles are for Use

The world is a very busy place and there are many more managers than one might first imagine. Each one of them needs to know what this book has to say. They need to know what works.

The examples found in the pages of this book were based on hard-won practical experience. They were not dreamed up in a back room somewhere. The technology described here works. It is to be used. The point is this: business is for people, so a powerful new technology of management should be for people as well. This one is.

Putting the Concepts Together

Management itself cannot be described by one or two simple maxims such as "Quality" or "Time Management." A true understanding of management requires familiarity with many interrelated concepts, each of which must stand the test of workability.

The subject may appear far-reaching and complex unless each concept is grasped by itself, as a simplicity. Then, when all the parts are brought together, they form a cohesive, useful foundation of knowledge from which one can tackle any business situation.

You Need Training

This book only scratches the surface of a very complete and powerful technology of management. In order to take full control of the subject there is a great deal of study that must be done. However, it is time well spent.

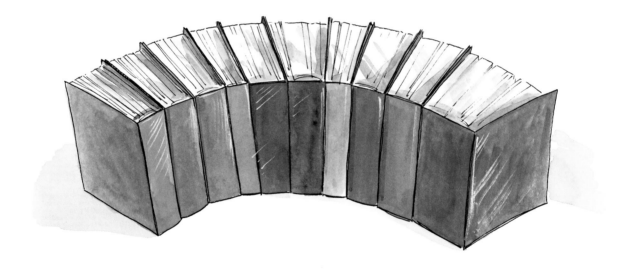

A very comprehensive understanding can be gained from the many courses available from Hubbard Colleges of Administration and licensed Hubbard Management Consultants around the world.

Philosophical Summary

Advancing a Culture

Business management in some way affects every waking or sleeping minute of everyone's life. There is no getting around this point. It does not matter how advanced or primitive the culture.

Whether you are dealing with a caveman society or an intergalactic star fleet, the underlying realities of management covered in this book will apply.

Social Implications of the Product

Sadly, a great many of the products of today's businesses do not benefit even their customers much less the rest of society. Too often a group's marketing genius, legal expertise and organizational and financial resources are used to trick or mislead.

Nevertheless, it is a most fascinating fact that the laws of running an organization apply to any group, business or government regardless of its goals, products or social value.

What Does the Future Hold?

This book proposes a set of standards which are desperately needed in today's businesses internationally. It was written with the sole purpose of helping to cause broad social improvement by increasing mankind's general understanding of how to get things done as individuals, as managers and as a team.

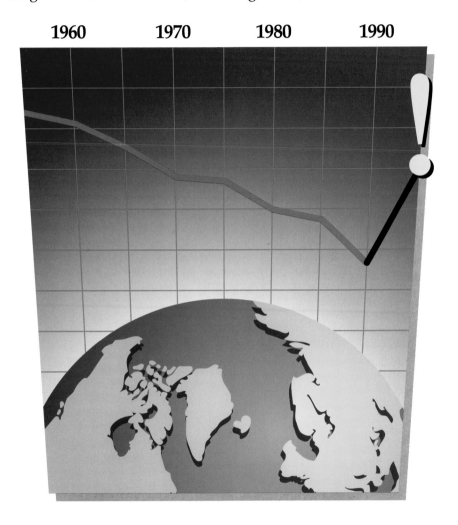

How far can all this take us? What degree of stable, balanced economic growth is possible for our planet? One thing is certain, wherever a business's products are truly worthwhile, it is in everyone's best interest to see the business flourish and prosper. Decay, once begun, can accelerate quickly. However, the reverse is also true. It is up to you and your colleagues to turn things around.

As you begin to gain a broader understanding of L. Ron Hubbard's writings on management, you will greatly appreciate the fact that he was indeed...

speaking from experience!

The End!

Glossary

ACCOUNTING   The action of noting down, classifying, ensuring the accuracy of, evaluating and interpreting the financial facts and figures of an organization or business.

ADMIN SCALE   The administrative scale, or admin scale, gives a sequence and relative seniority of subjects relating to organization. It is a guide used to establish and align the activities inherent in any successful organization.

AFFLUENCE   An affluence condition exists when there is a steep increase in a statistic (such as sudden peaks of income).

BACKLOG   An increasing accumulation of unperformed tasks. Backlogs are a strong indicator that something is very wrong with the production in that area. (See also DONES) Backlogs occur for various reasons. But the two main classes are (1) NOT-DONES and (2) HALF-DONES.

BATTLE PLAN   A battle plan, or BP, is sometimes referred to as a game plan. A BP is a list of targets for the coming day or week which forwards the strategic plan and handles the immediate factors which impede it. More than just a "to do" list, its actions align with the strategies of the group.

BEAN THEORY   The concept of spending money (beans) to make more money (more beans). The term comes from an example of farming beans. A farmer uses a handful of beans to grow an entire crop of beans. The resulting crop has far more value than the original handful. However, other "beans" are used as well (labor, fertilizer, equipment). When the value of the beans that were spent is compared to the value of the beans that were produced, a profit should be shown.

COMMUNICATION   The interchange of ideas, individual to individual, individual to group, group to individual, and group to group. (See COMMUNICATION FORMULA)

227

Glossary

COMMUNICATION FORMULA The formula of communication is: cause, distance, effect, with intention, attention, and duplication (the action of reproducing something exactly) with understanding.

CONDITION An operating state. (See CONDITION FORMULA, SCALE OF CONDITIONS)

CONDITION FORMULA Each one of the conditions from Confusion through Power and Power Change has its own specific formula. Each formula is a precise conceptual outline of the steps that need to be taken in order to bring the area (to which the formula is being applied) into the next higher condition.

CONFUSION, CONDITION OF When in a condition of Confusion, the person or area will be in a state of random motion. There will be no real production, only disorder and confusion.

COSTING A detailed listing of the costs of an area, activity or action. This includes premises, pay of personnel, estimates of legal fees and every other sub-product which must be acquired or performed to achieve the product.

DANGER, CONDITION OF A Danger condition exists when: (A) statistics show a continuing steady decline, or (B) a statistic plunges downward very steeply, or (C) a senior executive finds himself doing the job of another activity because that area is in trouble. Any situation in Danger is dangerous because if the activity or area were to continue in a danger condition it would simply cease to exist as a producing entity.

DATA Facts, graphs, statements, decisions, actions and descriptions which are supposedly true.

DEPARTMENT The org board contains seven divisions which describe all the actions encompassed by the organization. Each division is subdivided into three departments. In these seven divisions and their twenty-one departments, one finds all the functions, duties, positions, sequences of action, and command channels of the organization. (See ORG BOARD)

DEVELOPED TRAFFIC "Developed" traffic does not mean usual and necessary traffic. It means unusual and unnecessary traffic. It is created (developed), inapplicable, unhandled work (traffic). It is referred to as Developed Traffic, or Dev-T, because it develops more work unnecessarily for anyone involved.

DIVISION The org board contains seven divisions which describe all the actions encompassed by the organization. Each division is subdivided into three departments. In these seven divisions and their twenty-one departments, one finds all the functions, duties, positions, sequences of action, and command channels of the organization. (See ORG BOARD)

DONES When a product is gotten, it is done. (Compare with BACKLOGS, HALF-DONES, and NOT-DONES)

DOUBT, CONDITION OF When one cannot make up one's mind as to an individual, group, organization or project, a condition of Doubt exists.

DOWN STATISTIC When the quantity of production decreases, this is called a down statistic. (See STATISTICS)

ECHELON A level of command in an organization. For example, the high-ranking executives are referred to as the upper echelon.

ECONOMY The management of the use of the income, products and resources of a country, state, group, etc.

EMERGENCY, CONDITION OF An Emergency condition is represented by statistics that are unchanging or trending downward. When things are worsening they must be corrected. If the right actions are not taken then things can really fall apart. Things either expand or they contract. They do not remain level in this universe. Further, when something seeks to remain level and unchanged, it contracts. Therefore an unchanging statistic, as well as one that is worsening, are both in Emergency.

ENEMY, CONDITION OF When a person is an avowed and knowing enemy of an individual, group, project or organization, a condition of Enemy exists.

Glossary

EXCHANGE   The process of offering something valuable in return for some other valuable. Exchange does not always involve money as one of the valuables. For example, someone may offer their help regarding one activity in exchange for help on some other activity.

EXISTING SCENE   The current situation in a business, good or bad. (Compare to IDEAL SCENE)

EXPENSE   The financial cost or price involved in some activity.

FACT   Something that can be proven to exist by visible evidence.

FINANCE   That area of a business concerned with maintaining the inflow of money greater than the outflow, and with the management of money.

GOAL   A dream or vision of a desirable future that is put forth and which acts as an overall guide regarding the activities of a person or group. The overall concept of what one intends to accomplish.

HALF-DONE   An incomplete task or product. (Compare with BACKLOG)

HANDLING   What one does to correct the scene. It is the implementation of the solution. When the handling is complete, the situation will have been corrected and will no longer exist.

HAT   A "hat" is the duty or duties of a certain post. The term "hat" originated from the fact that posts are often distinguished by the type of hat worn.

HAT WRITE-UP   A complete summary of the exact duties of a particular post.

HATTING   Hatting is the action done to train someone on the duties of their post/hat. (See HAT)

IDEAL SCENE   The vision of the way a business or any of its parts ideally should be. (Compare to EXISTING SCENE) A description of the ideal scene always coincides 100% with the goals and purposes of an activity.

INCOME   The sum total of money that a company or business receives from all sources as a result of business transactions; also called gross income.

INSOLVENT   When an organization or part of an organization has expenses greater than its income. This would be represented by a crossed cash-bills statistic (more bills than cash on hand to pay them).

INTENTION   Intention is the idea that one is going to accomplish something. If you intend something to happen, it happens. Verbalization is not the intention. The intention is the carrier wave which takes the verbalization along with it.

INVESTIGATION   The careful discovery and sorting of facts.

LEADERSHIP   Leadership is based almost solely on the ability to give and enforce orders. True leadership is found in those who can keep the goals and purposes alive in every member of the group.

LIABILITY, CONDITION OF   Liability is assigned where careless or malicious and knowing damage is caused to projects, organizations or activities. It is adjudicated that it is malicious and knowing because orders have been published against it or because it is contrary to the intentions and actions of the remainder of the team or the purpose of the project or organization.

MANAGEMENT   A science governed by specific principles and procedures which, if applied, will improve the existing scene.

MANAGEMENT BY STATISTICS   A technique of management using statistics. The most direct observation in an organization (or a country) is statistics. They measure what is done. It cannot be said too often that management is best done by statistics. Management by statistics works only if: the statistics are collected (always and without fail), the statistics which are reported are accurate, and the appropriate statistics are tracked foreach area.

Glossary

MANAGER   One who both follows and enforces the policies of the group. A manager is there to ensure that results occur. It is the responsibility of a manager to see that those things in his areas which are started get completed.

MONEY   Money is only something that can be exchanged confidently for goods or services. It is a symbol which represents value in terms of goods or services.

MORALE   A sense of common purpose or a degree of dedication to a common task in a particular group or organization. Morale is made up of high purpose and mutual confidence.

NON-EXISTENCE, CONDITION OF   When an area doesn't produce any valuable final products (or is non-viable) it is in the condition of Non-Existence. It is labeled Non-Existence because it isn't producing (as if it didn't exist).

NORMAL, CONDITION OF   A Normal condition is represented by a routine or gradual increase in a statistic. It is called Normal because things are running well, the results are neither stellar nor poor, they are steadily increasing, which is good (normal).

NOT-DONE   A task not done or product not produced. (Compare with BACKLOG)

OPINION Something which may or may not be based on any facts. (Compare to FACT). An opinion is an attitude, concept or belief one has about something.

ORDER   Orders involve specific actions which get things done. They can and should be done in a short period of time (NOW).

ORG BOARD   Hats and posts must be coordinated within an organization in order to achieve maximum efficiency and results. The organizing board (org board for short) is used to actively organize and control the flows of communication, command and production in a business. An org board reduces confusion. It tells everyone what to expect from everyone else.

ORGANIZATION   The act of organizing or the process of being organized. An organization is made up of associated individuals who have an agreed-upon goal or intention.

PLAN An outline of the general actions which a group must execute in order to achieve its goals. Plans are sometimes referred to as "strategic plans," " business plans," "five-year plans," etc.

POST An assigned or appointed position, job or duty.

POWER CHANGE There are only two circumstances which require replacement, the very successful one or the very unsuccessful one. Power Change involves the steps one would take when replacing another who had the post (or area) in a Power condition. Power Change ensures that the stellar results will continue.

POWER, CONDITION OF Power is being able to do what one is doing when one is doing it. A power condition is represented by a statistic that has gone into a very high range. It is a normal trend in a brand-new range. It is called power because there is such an abundance of production that momentary halts or dips cannot pull it down or imperil its survival.

PRICING Establishing the value in terms of money of a product or service offered for sale.

PRODUCT A completed thing that has exchange value within or outside the activity. (See also VALUABLE FINAL PRODUCT)

PRODUCTION The activity of providing a product or service.

PROGRAMME A series of steps in the correct sequence necessary to carry out a plan. A single plan may be broken down into many programmes. (See PLAN) The British spelling of "programme" is used to avoid possible confusion with a computer "program."

PROJECT The sequence of steps written to carry out one step of a programme. (See PROGRAMME)

PURPOSE The lesser goal applying to specific activities or subjects. Purposes address more specific subjects or activities than goals. (See GOAL)

QUOTA A quota is the number assigned to whatever is to be produced. It is a future expectancy.

Glossary

SCALE OF CONDITIONS   The different condition formulas make up a scale which shows the condition or state, which is to say the degree of success or survival of an individual, his post, a division, a continental area or international area at any one particular time and as compared to other times.

SOLVENCY   The condition of being solvent. The basic rule of solvency is "income must be greater than outgo."

STATISTICS   A statistic, or stat, is a number or amount compared to an earlier number or amount of the same thing. Stats refer to the quantity of work done or the value of it in money.

STRATEGIC PLANNING   A statement of intended plans for accomplishing a broad objective. It is the central strategy worked out at the top which, like an umbrella, covers the activities of the echelons below it. (Compare with TACTICAL PLANNING)

STRATEGY   The broad fashion of how things are to be conducted. (Compare with TACTICS)

SUB-PRODUCT   Each part of a production sequence is called a sub-product. There are often many steps which go into the completion of a single product. (See VALUABLE FINAL PRODUCT)

TACTICAL PLANNING   Tactical planning takes the broad targets laid out in a strategic plan and breaks them down into precise and exactly-targeted actions called programmes and projects. (Compare with STRATEGIC PLANNING)

TACTICS   Specific and immediate objectives. (Compare with STRATEGY)

TARGET   A target is an objective one intends to accomplish in a given period of time.

TRAFFIC   The daily activities of any normal business (such as communications, people, paperwork, motion and the like) is referred to as traffic.

TREASON, CONDITION OF   Treason is defined as betrayal after trust.

TREND   The overall measure of expansion (production) or contraction (non-production) over several weeks or even months.

UP STATISTIC   When the quantity of production increases, this is called an up statistic. (See STATISTICS)

VALUABLE FINAL PRODUCT   A valuable final product, or VFP, is a completed product (goods or services) that has value to others and can be exchanged with others.

VALUE   Anything which is needed and wanted has value, meaning it is worth something to someone.

If you would like additional books, or want more information on the technology presented in this book, call the number below.

For additional copies of **Speaking From Experience,** call the number below and we will direct you to the bookstore in your area with copies in stock.

If there is no convenient location for you, we will gladly take your order by phone and ship you as many copies as you need. Discounts are available for bulk orders.

Concept Technologies, Inc.

1-800-BOOK-255
Advanced Concept Communication Techniques
www.speakingfromexperience.net